In memory of Mike

In the steps of
- 1767 -
Perambulation

History
& Hikes
of the ancient
Royal Hunting
Forest of Knaresborough

by
Mike Brough

The story of Knaresborough's ancient
Royal Hunting Forest and a selection of circular walks
of different lengths with details of the exact locations of
all the remaining Boundary Stones.

ISBN: 978-0-9576091-0-5

Printed by:
Harrogate Printing Limited
Ripon Way, Harrogate, North Yorkshire

Published by:
Colin Michael Brough
142 West End Avenue, Harrogate, N Yorkshire HG2 9BT

To purchase please contact: historyandhikes@gmail.com

Cover image: Boundary Stone 11, Lippersley Pike

All profits from this book will be donated to Cancer Services at Harrogate and District NHS Foundation Trust. Such donations will be used to further improve support and comfort for patients having treatment for cancer and blood disorders.
Registered Charity Number: 1050008

Index

The Long Walks

A Very Long Walk

Appendices

List of Illustrations

Foreword

Early in his reign in 1357 Edward III visited Yorkshire and set aside a day for some hunting in the nearby Forest of Knaresborough. The royal party found a wild boar and set off in pursuit on horseback. Catching up with it, a member of the king's party threw a spear, which wounded the animal: harried by the dogs, it turned round and charged straight at the king's horse. The terrified animal deposited the king on the ground, right in the path of the advancing boar. Had it not been for the quick thinking and courage of my ancestor, circuit judge Thomas Ingleby, who charged in and killed the enraged animal, the king would in all probability have suffered fatal wounds, and his reign would have been drawn to a tragic and premature conclusion. Thomas Ingleby was knighted and he and his family were granted a charter to hold a weekly market in Ripley and an annual fair 'on the eve of the day and the morrow of the Assumption of the Blessed Virgin Mary'. Finally, he and his successors were granted the right of free warren: the right to hunt anywhere in the Forest of Knareborough – a prerogative shared only with the king and his family.

The Forest of Knaresborough was then and is today a very special area: a place of beauty, a place of romance, of kingly sport, of history and legend. In some areas it has probably changed very little since the days of Edward III, in others the human presence is far more invasive. Several landmarks – tracks, woods and bridges, mentioned in the historical account have survived and are still familiar to us today. Above all, enjoy the natural beauty that surrounds you as you follow in the footesteps of those stalwart men who trod the same path as they completed their perambulation of the forest. Michael Brough has brought the Royal Hunting Forest of Knaresborough back to life, and for that he richly deserves our gratitude.

Sir Thomas Ingilby of Ripley Castle

Acknowledgements

There have been a number of people who have assisted in one way or another with the compilation of this book, to whom I am very grateful. First and foremost is my wife, Dorrie who has accompanied me on many of the walks, and between us we have made notes which have formed the basis of my descriptions. My daughter, Helen for her encouragement and support together with feedback on walks she has field tested for me. I have also had the pleasure of completing many of these walks in the company of others, who have usually carried a hard copy of the walk descriptions and have commented as and when they have felt that confusion could arise. I have sat around a table with some of these and discussed options as to how the work ought to be presented, and for this I would like to thank Bill Osborne and Peter Wood. Some of the walks have been undertaken by individuals alone using these very descriptions and, as they have been very experienced walkers, their advice has been invaluable. They include Alasdair Maclean, Keith Wadd, Rodney Waddilove and John Hardy.

I owe a debt of gratitude to Cyril Mason of Ripon who showed me the location of many of the remaining Boundary Stones. He and John Webster had done much research and, although sadly John died before I embarked on this book and I never had the pleasure of meeting him, credit is rightly due to him. I have frequently spoken to William B Houseman whose knowledge of Nidderdale and its people is unequalled, and from him I have been able to add the colour of the recent past to the book.

Lydia Thomson has been heavily involved with editing and the layout of the work so that it is printer ready. My son, Julian has also put much work into the general design of the book, and also the design of the book's cover, and for that I am very much indebted.

I have gained a huge amount of pleasure in compiling this book. There have been many farmers and land owners who have supported and helped in different ways: Mark Smith of High Rails Farm and Andrew Walmsley of Scarah Bank Farm in the erection of Boundary Stone 42, Mervin Liddle at Sun Rise Farm Kirkby Overblow regarding access, and many others who have told me so much about life in the Forest today. Sir Thomas Ingilby of Ripley Castle whose family have been part of the Forest story from its beginning and both Ripley and Clint Parish Councils, have all played a part. I hope that I have remembered everyone, but I can say with certainty, thanks to you all.

A Personal Message

Having lived and worked in the locality of Knaresborough Forest for the last 40 years I found this book fascinating reading. Mike Brough must be commended for giving so much of his time to recording the history of Knaresborough Forest and indeed is carrying on the tradition of passing down his knowledge for future generation in a modern format.

I feel privileged to have met the author and to have been able to play a small part in this work. I hope you will all be able to enjoy the area of outstanding beauty during the walks Mike has documented and continue the tradition of passing down the Knaresborough Forest story.

Mark Smith, High Rails Farm, Ripley

Introduction

This book has been written with a number of objectives that I hope will match the interests of the various groups of people who may want to use it.

For those who are interested in the history of Knaresborough and the surrounding countryside, the first section describes the origins, and rise and fall of the Forest of Knaresborough, a vast area of moorland and woodland of 30,000 acres, and includes a description of some of the different Perambulations of its boundaries which were made over the centuries.

The second section is for those who want to get out and see the sites and sights of the ancient Forest for themselves. There is a series of 12 Short Walks of about 5 miles, with full details of how to follow each one, and each illustrated with a sketch map. After that, come 12 Long Walks, of around 10 miles, similarly described. All the Walks also include snippets of historical information, which I hope will make the way more interesting. The Walks follow rights of way, or permissive paths, or are on 'open access' land. However, if you wish to visit all of the existing Stones (which mark the Boundary of the Forest), you will need to ask permission from the landowner, for those on private land. Full details of all the Stones are included in an appendix at the end of the book. Many of the Walks follow sections of the Boundary, and pass by several of the Stones, but the final section describes the dream of a very long walk that follows the complete Boundary, and gives a detailed description of where the Boundary runs.

The book has a number of pencil sketches of places I found appealing, and hope that some of you may find them a worthwhile embellishment. There are a number of photographs of places and Stones you will pass, and as the

A stile near Thruscross

whole area is a lovely part of the country I hope these will serve as a reminder, in the wet winter months, of the Walks. I would like to think that this work may lead to a generation of walkers, historians and the general public, who will themselves become a part of the revival of interest in a now almost forgotten Royal Hunting Forest, and restore it to its rightful place as one of the most important and interesting areas of Yorkshire. If you find any of the missing Boundary Stones while doing the walks, do please let me know!

Map Legend

 Line of Forest Boundary

 Water

Knaresborough and its Royal Hunting Forest

A history

Knaresborough is situated on a high plateau of magnesium limestone rock above the Nidd gorge. The town was formerly known as Chenaresburg, and it was closely associated with Isurium (now known as Aldborough) in the days of the Brigante tribes before the Roman occupation. The defeat of the Brigante tribes by the Romans happened about the year AD 50, and the Roman occupation then lasted for 400 years. There are still the remains of Brigantian defensive earthworks to be seen in Haverah Park at Bank Slack, which are almost 2000 years old! After the Romans left in about AD 450 there was a 600-year period of uncertainty and danger when the people were left vulnerable to invasion by the Saxons, the Danes, the Vikings and the Norse. After the Battle of Hastings in 1066 the Normans set about establishing their rule, and as they moved further north they no doubt saw the strategic advantage of the Knaresborough Castle site, easily defended with 100-foot cliffs on three sides. They soon appointed Serlo d' Burgh and later Eustace Fitz John as its governors. Prior to this there was probably only a wooden defence, but a more substantial castle was built and extended during the rule of a succession of governors.

Much of the North up to this time was in the hands of Danish and Saxon thanes, including Archil and Gamell, who were antagonised by the harsh and often unjust Norman rule, and eventually there was a rebellion, which was quickly suppressed. William sent his army north in reprisal, in an

The Forest of Knaresborough

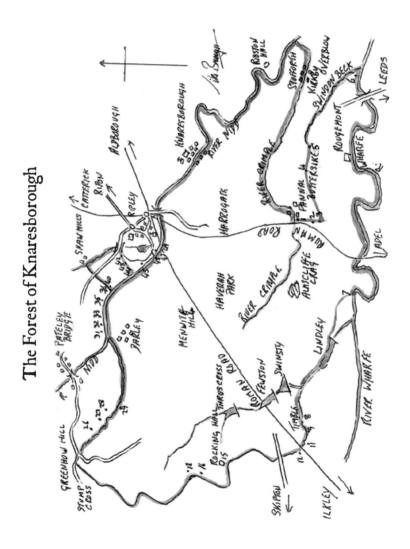

action known as the 'Harrying of the North'. William's armies killed all, including women and children, and destroyed their houses and farms and even livestock. There was no one left even to bury the dead, and the land was laid waste. Eventually, probably during the reign of Henry II (1154-1189) some of that wasteland, now partially re-populated and with re-established tree-cover, was used as a royal hunting forest. The Normans, and subsequently the Plantagenets, were passionately fond of hunting and much of England was turned over to forests. This did not necessarily mean trees, but rather a specific area in which wild game could be preserved for the princely sport of hunting. During the 12th and 13th centuries a total of 65 royal hunting forests, chases, and deer parks were established, amounting to approximately a third of the land mass of England. Knaresborough Forest was extensive, covering over 20,000 'forest acres'. This equates to 30,000 modern acres, and extended from Little Ribston to Poole and up to Greenhow and Stump Cross. Within this area there were two specific parts which were fenced off in an ingenious way with palings, maintained by local people known as Foresters, which allowed game to get in but not to get back out, essentially confining game to specific areas. These were Haverah Park to the west of Beckwithshaw, and Bilton Park on the west side of Knaresborough. The penalties for anyone taking game or even wood from royal Forests were very severe, although desperation did drive people to take the risk. There was another hunting park associated with Knaresborough, although not in the forest, called Hey-a-Park to the east of the town. These three Parks were used at different times for the breeding of 'venison', and for horses. The ancient word 'venison' was used to describe all of the game of the forest.

There is considerable doubt as to exactly when the ancient Forest of Knaresborough was formed, but some light has been thrown on the subject by several local historians. Some link the foundation with Hugh de Moreville, one of the knights implicated in the murder of Thomas à Becket, the Primate of All England, in December 1170. De Moreville was the Constable of the Castle and Liberty of Knaresborough and after the crime the four murderers, Fitzurse, de Tracy, le Bret, and de Moreville, fled first to Saltwood Castle, then to South Malling and finally to Knaresborough. It is possible that, by establishing the Royal Hunting Forest of Knaresborough, de Moreville hoped to regain the favour of the King, whose loyal supporter he was, as the Forest certainly dates back to around this period. All four murderers were excommunicated by the Pope, but later pardoned providing they went on a pilgrimage to Jerusalem, and all four died on their journey to the Holy Land. It is said that, before he set out, de Moreville built the first church at Hampsthwaite, where there is a lane which is still known as Thomas à Becket Way.

Other historians, particularly William Grainge in his works on the district towards the end of the 19th century, credit William de Stutville with the establishment of the Forest around the year 1177, when he was Governor of Knaresborough Castle, where he remained with his family until 1204. Knaresborough Forest was particularly popular with Henry II (reigned 1154-1189) and also with King John (1199-1216) who loved the thrill of the chase. It is said that John gave out the first 'Maundy Money' in Knaresborough. In 1205 Brian de l'Isle became King's custodian, and in 1229 Hubert de Burgh. The King (Henry III, 1216-1272) took over the custody himself in 1233, and then granted the whole of the Honour of Knaresborough, including the Forest, to his brother the Earl of Cornwall. Cornwall's son then took it over until his death in 1275. In 1307 King Edward II granted the Honour to a Frenchman, Piers Gaveston, one of his favourites. Gaveston was disliked by some of the most powerful lords of the land, in particular the Duke of Lancaster and the Nevilles of Warwick including 'Guy the King Maker', and was driven back to Gascony, but later was recalled by Edward II. He met an untimely death in 1312.

After the Battle of Bannockburn in 1314, the whole of the Forest and surrounding area was devastated for many years by attacks led by Robert the Bruce and the Black Douglas. The Scots were getting their own back for the scourge of the foreign policy of Edward I, 'Hammer of the Scots', and were aided by the subsequent weakness of Edward II. There are still scorch marks in the tower of Knaresborough Parish Church and charred remains of old buildings are excavated in the town from time to time.

Edward III (1327-1377) settled the Honour of Knaresborough on his wife Philippa, who held it to her death in 1369. Edward then granted the whole of Knaresborough Castle, the Honour, the Liberty, and the Forest to his son John of Gaunt, Duke of Lancaster. There still remain the ruins of what is now thought to have been a hunting lodge near to Beaver Dyke Reservoir in Haverah Park known as John o' Gaunt's Castle, although it probably actually predates John of Gaunt. The Honour has remained in the ownership of the Duchy of Lancaster ever since, with the Queens of both Charles I and II, Henrietta Maria and Catherine of Braganza, holding it in dower. During the 15th century, Thomas Chaucer, the nephew of Geoffrey Chaucer, was Constable of the Forest, an office which was ended as recently as 1916.

The end of the Forest

The Forest had, for a long period, outgrown its original purpose, as the Norman and Plantagenet passion for hunting was not shared by successive royal dynasties. The Tudors may have enjoyed the chase but not with the same enthusiasm, and in the time of the Stuarts, and later the Hanoverians, other issues took priority. Certain rights had been granted to local yeoman farmers who were known as Copyholders. Although the established customs of the Forest forbade it, they had sublet their privilege to others for a consideration. In some cases the sub-lessees too had sublet, until the system was no longer viable. The result was that, in order to improve their living, these Foresters began to engage in other industries, the main ones being flax growing and linen milling. Many of the ancient Forest corn mills were converted into water-powered flax mills with various end-products such as twine, rope and linen. The number of mills increased, with almost every tributary of the main dales providing power. These operated legally within the Forest, although not within the original meaning of 'hunting forest law'. Other industries also grew up during this period. Iron ore was mined in a number of parts of the Forest and was smelted at Cinder Hills near Darley, at Kirkby Overblow, and in the Crimple Valley. Penny Pot Lane leading west out of Harlow Hill in Harrogate was once called Iron Gate Lane. A fine single-arch packhorse bridge called the Iron Gate Bridge still crosses Oak Beck. Limestone was quarried and burnt to make slaked lime to be used as fertiliser on the land, as a form of cement, and as a wash to put on walls and on the edges of the Forest, lead and stone were quarried too. There were several places in and on the edge of the Forest such as Bilton Park, Smelthouse Gill, and Brow Wood, Thornthwaite, where coal was mined, though this was poor-quality brown coal known as

The Perambulations

Over the life of the Forest it was customary to 'beat the bounds' at intervals, to establish and re-establish the legal boundaries. A number of these Perambulations are on record, and a list is given in Appendix 2. The transcribed texts of two, that of 1576 and the 'Last Perambulation of 1767', are given as Appendices 3 and 4. The two are remarkably similar, but the Elizabethan Perambulation is of interest for its colourful old wording.

The Last Perambulation of Knaresborough Forest took place three years before the Enclosure Act, on the 3rd September 1767. A group of interested individuals gathered at the confluence of the River Crimple with the River Nidd, near to Walshford. Half a dozen officials were present:

Joseph Tullie, Receiver General of the Revenues of the Duchy of Lancaster,

Robert Roper, Auditor for the Northern Parts of the Duchy,

William Ashurst, Auditor for the Southern Parts of the Duchy,

William Masterman, Clerk of the Council,

William Marsden, Surveyor of the Lands,

Francis Russell, Surveyor of the Woods.

They proclaimed to officials from the Castle, including the Deputy Constable and the Deputy Bailiff, and to a number of interested parties such as copyholders and tenants, and to some old people who would have remembered earlier 'Perambulations' and were conversant with the neighbourhood, that they were empowered by Royal Commission to establish the 'Metes and Boundaries' of the Forest. The party took three weeks working continuously to complete the Perambulation, finishing on

27th September, when they described the boundary of the Forest on three skins of vellum and put their signatures to it.

The Boundary Stones which they set up to prescribe the exact area were large and impressive, each numbered from 1 to 49 and marked K-F 1767. Thus it is possible to identify not only the Boundary, but which Stones are still to be found and those which have been lost. Appendix 1 includes a list of all the known Stones, with grid references, and notes on access. Several of the original boundary stones have at different times been replaced. Stones 8 and 9 have the date 1825 and must be replacements. Stone 33 was found in the river and re-erected by John Webster and Cyril Mason, with the help of a historical group. Stone 42, which disappeared about 20 years ago, was replaced by myself with support from two local business men / farmers. The Walks in the second section of this book follow as closely as possible the original boundary of the Forest, and I hope that they will inspire you to look at the old Stones, and perhaps to uncover others. I still hope that the missing Stones may yet be found, or replaced by those who care.

The Challenges

While proof reading for my book it crossed my mind that tucked away as long term projects it is possible to identify challenges here. Without going into detail I thought I might flag suggestions up for readers' consideration.

By looking at the sections of the book marked the Very Long Walk I am convinced that given time and care it might be possible to create an excellent new National Long Distance Walk in the Harrogate area on a par with Offa's Dyke, the Lyke Wake Walk and others. The round walk would be approximately 90 miles and would cover a wonderfully diverse variety of countryside.

Another challenge might be to re-discover the locations of some or indeed all of the Stones identified as missing, and if appropriate organise their replacements and even their re-erection.

A distinctly more technical problem might well involve specialist skills, and that would be to attempt to locate the position of Stone 6. I believe it is probably in 35 feet of water somewhere near to the point where Swindon Beck flows into the River Wharfe. I believe that if this is the case the nearby farmer might be willing to assist using heavy tractor lifting equipment.

It is my hope that this book will inspire a whole new range of walkers who share an interest in local history to put Knaresborough Forest back where it belongs… 'identified' as an outstandingly beautiful and interesting part of our heritage that offers those with a wide diversity of interest a sound basis upon which to develop new paths.

The Walks

The following sections describe 12 Short Walks (of around 5 miles) and 12 Long Walks (of around 10 miles) that investigate different areas of the Forest, its Boundary, and the Boundary Stones. The detailed description for each Walk is preceded by a paragraph saying how long the walk is, and giving a brief overview, how to find the starting point (with a grid reference) and how it relates to the Boundary, and any Stones that it passes. Also included are the names of any useful pubs to be found on or near the route! Each walk also has a sketch map, which should help you find your way. This is intended as an indication only and is not necessarily drawn to scale, so I recommend that an Ordnance Survey Map (1:25000) and a compass is always carried. If there is any doubt about 'which way now?', or 'what is that hill over there?', then these will always be useful. As well as the route description I have included little items of historical interest, some of which you might not have known about. So remember to take the book with you too! If you are new to walking, you might find the notes below useful.

Notes for new walkers

What to take with you (as well as map, book and compass):

A **first aid kit** is a sensible precaution. They are cheap, and just a small one is all you need. Carry a day sack (small rucksack) with some **survival rations,** for example a picnic if you have chosen one of the longer walks, and also emergency food such as chocolate or raisins. These are high in energy, and just in case there has been an accident and one of the party can only make slow progress, or worse has to wait for help, they will sustain. The same sort of considerations apply if the weather deteriorates and you get lost. Also take a **plastic bottle** containing fluid, water or fruit juice, or a **flask** with a hot drink in winter. Keep in your day sack a **pair of waterproof over trousers** and **extra warm clothing**. It is best to choose several thin layers rather than one thick one. You should always have a **weather-proof anorak**, either on or packed. Always wear good, sturdy and comfortable **boots or shoes**, and two pairs of socks, one thin and one thick.

Children and Dogs

Be aware that children do not develop a proper energy metabolism until they are about twenty, so it is important that they are not subjected to walks that may be beyond their capabilities. Dogs can become distressed in hot weather, and it is a good idea to carry a water supply for them. Most of the walks described in this book will involve walking through fields with animals, and care needs to be exercised where there are cattle, especially with calves. In winter many farmers bring their cattle in, so you may not encounter them then.

Country Code

1. If walking on country roads it is a good idea to face oncoming traffic.
2. The country is a working environment and so avoid interference with farm animals, stock and machinery.
3. Use gates and stiles to cross fences and walls.
4. Close gates unless they have obviously been left open.
5. Do not risk fire in any way, and do not drop cigarette ends.
6. Do not drop litter. If you have brought items in wrappers, then take the wrappers home.
7. Go quietly, you will see far more.

8. Keep your dog on a lead especially on roads or near livestock, and always take a supply of plastic bags to clean up after it, and dispose of them properly. Dog faeces cause terrible problems with cows and sheep, almost always ending in their death.

9. Do not pollute water supplies.

10. Keep to paths

Please note that the shooting season begins on 4th August and many of the 'Right to Roam Moors' will then be closed to walkers for a period of two months. Check before planning a walk in the high moorland areas prior to setting off.

Important note

Walking in the countryside will always carry the risk of an accident. Neither the author nor the publisher can accept any responsibility, and those using this book for walks must take proper care at all times.

The
Short
Walks

Short Walk 1

Little Ribston - Plumpton

Distance: **6.25 miles**   *Map:* **OS Explorer 289**

Description: Easy going underfoot and generally level, muddy in winter, especially along the banks of the Crimple.

Starting Point: **SE 386532**
In the middle of Little Ribston, at the junction of the unclassified road to Spofforth with the B6164 Knaresborough to Wetherby road.

Boundary Notes: The Boundary in this area follows the River Nidd downstream to the Crimple, and then upstream along the Crimple.

1. Follow the road towards Spofforth for a third of a mile, and where the road bends left take the sign-posted track along a field side to the right. After two fields, the track becomes a path and continues beside a large hedge until it passes the water treatment works on the left. At the top of the treatment works the path turns first to the left, and then in a few yards right, leaving the works behind. Continue along the edge of the field through three fields and down York Hill to the Harrogate-Wetherby road (A661). Follow this to the left towards Wetherby for 250 yards, keeping on the grass verge as the road is busy and the traffic is fast, and then enter the farm yard of Crosper Farm.

2. Walk straight ahead past several farm buildings and at the end, where a huge new barn has recently been built, turn left and make for a heavy gate

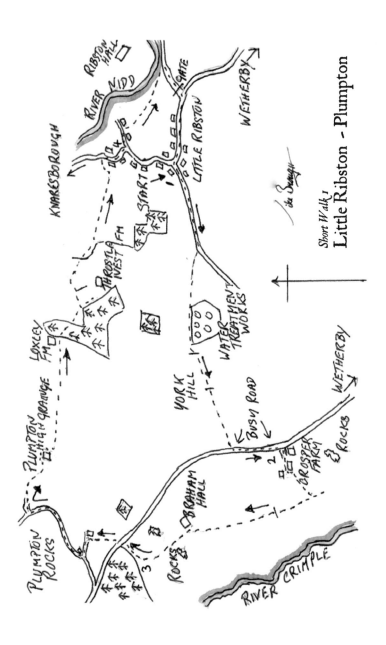

to the right. Go through this, being sure to close the gate behind you. (NB. Animals getting onto the A661 would be very dangerous; farm yards are also dangerous for children). Go directly down the field to a gate at the bottom where there is a stile on the left. Do not take the stile, but go to the right, keeping the field boundary on your left, to reach a gate ahead and continue, past an old water storage pool, to the right-hand corner of the field and into the next field by a dyke. The footpath leads up the hill towards Braham Hall and past its lower boundary. Continue on this line past a series of impressive rock outcrops towards a wood called The Warren.

The outcrops of rock are millstone grit and, like Plumpton Rocks, they are the remains of the delta of a river, the estuary of which was in this area at a time when the world's tectonic plates were in a very different position. They may well have been covered for millions of years and then exposed by the action of more recent ice ages.

The Plumpton Estate was bought by Daniel Lascelles soon after the death of Robert Plumpton in 1749. Plumpton Rocks was developed later by Edmond the 1st Earl of Harewood, as a 'Romantic Garden', and was painted by J.W. Turner on more than one occasion.

3. Follow the wood side up to the A661 and cross it directly to another path that leads into the tiny village of Plumpton. Pass the houses and turn right into the drive of Plumpton Hall at the lodge. Walk along the drive towards what remains of the Hall and at a junction sign-posted to Loxley Farm, turn right. The farm track passes through the yard of Plumpton High Grange, past Loxley Farm and into Braham Wood. Go through the wood and directly to the left-hand corner of a wood ahead. Reaching this corner the path forks, and you take the left-hand path, keeping the field

Ribston Hall

boundary on the right. The path turns slightly left and then right, and then crosses two large fields to reach Little Ribston. After a left and right turn on the edge of the village, the path comes out onto the B6164.

4. Turn right, and where the road bends right turn left, along an unmade driveway past a house. The path unexpectedly now goes to the right off this and through a cottage garden into a field. The path crosses the field along a line of trees and through a gate to reach a bend in the river Nidd.

Watch out here for an excellent view of Ribston Hall. This beautiful house is the ancient seat of the Goodrick family, and is now the home of Mr and Mrs Charles Dent whose family have lived here since 1830. It was originally owned by the Knights Templar, and still contains their chapel. In the grounds there is a jousting field, the Ribston Pippin from which all pippin apples originate, and Saxon Hows (Peesbury and Maunbury) which may have been the burial place of those who fell in some dark-age battle. This was the place where the plot was hatched that led to the 'Bloodless Revolution', when the protestant William of Orange was invited to assume the English Throne and James II of the House of Stuart was deposed.

5. On reaching the river, turn right and follow the drive of Ribston Hall to the road back to the centre of the village and the starting place.

Hookstone Wood - Fulwith - Pannal

Distance: **5.5 miles**   *Map:* **OS Explorer 297 or 289**

Description: A comfortable, attractive, edge of town walk, gentle hills, unspoilt villages, and good going underfoot, although boots essential, especially in winter.

Pubs: The Harewood, Pannal; The Black Swan, Burn Bridge; The Woodlands, Harrogate.

Starting Point: **SE318545**
Hookstone Road on the south side of Harrogate. Off-street parking is possible on St Helen's Road or any of the other roads that lead off Hookstone Road. There is a regular bus service to this point from Harrogate Bus Station, and a train service from Harrogate Station to Hornbeam Park.

Boundary Notes: The Boundary in this area follows the River Crimple. The walk passes Stone 1.

1. Take the narrow, sign-posted footpath that leads between houses into Hookstone Wood. The path opens out into the wood in under 30 yards and continues straight ahead until reaching Hookstone Wood Ponds. There are boulders and fallen tree branches to indicate the path. At the ponds turn right, pass the wired boundary of the playing fields of St John Fisher School on the right and the edge of a disused quarry, now utilised by enterprising children who have created an amazing adventure cycle park on the left. Turn left on a track that in 25 yards bears right. This lovely woodland ends at a gate. Through this, follow the obvious track across the field to a stone bridge which goes over Hornbeam (a.k.a.Hookstone) Beck.

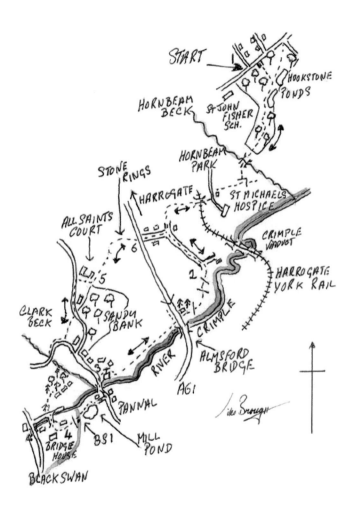

Short Walk 2
Hookstone Wood - Fulwith - Pannal

After the bridge, the track goes up a small grassy field and to a small gate into a footpath. Ignore the stile to the left (which leads into Bathing Well Wood and on to Crimple, see Short Walk 3), and turn right here, on the path leading up to the drive to Crimple House, St Michael's Hospice. Turn left past two cottages, and before the entrance of St Michael's Hospice grounds, turn right on a path that goes on over the Harrogate to Leeds Railway. In 200 yards there are signed footpaths off to the right but stay with the now tarmac road which bears left. A quarter of a mile on, bear left at the junction of Fulwith Mill Lane which comes in from the right and continue down the hill. The road swings left at the bottom of the hill to go on to the very old Fulwith Mill, but at this corner take the clearly signed track to the right. The track bears away left but do not follow it, instead keeping the hedge on your right go straight on. There is a 'bridle way' sign, and a rather dilapidated green metal sign marked 'Almsford Bank'.

Watch out for Red Kites, which are quite common in this district. They are easily distinguished from other birds of prey by their distinctive, deeply forked tails.

2. At the metal gate, continue across the field to another metal gate. Go through this and bear very slightly right across the next field. As you go over the brow of the small hill ahead, a wicket gate comes into view. Go through this and follow the obvious path with woodland to your right and a lovely view over Crimple Beck to the left. At the end of this path, pass former riding stables and exit onto the main road and the bottom of Almsford Bank. Be sure to close the gate securely behind you! Cross the road to a short lane directly opposite. At the bottom of the lane there is a path to the left which follows the River Crimple close by, and another that goes right leading up to Stone Rings Road. The path to the left is the

Boundary Stone 1

actual Boundary of Knaresborough Forest, but there is also one straight ahead that is a pleasant field path. Both of these lead to a stile into Pannal Church Yard.

3. After leaving the Church Yard, turn left and walk up the main street of Pannal and, after crossing the bridge over the River Crimple, turn right onto Mill Lane. This leads to the mill pond and onto a path that follows the line of the old mill race.

> *If you are very observant and look carefully to your left 10 yards or so before the scrubby woodland becomes a green field, you will (with difficulty) observe Stone 1. It is partially hidden by woodland debris, and is difficult to get to because what is left of the mill race flows between it and the path.*

4. Continue to where the drive of Bridge House is to the left, and then turn right to cross a stone bridge across the Crimple. On the other side of the lane ahead is a footpath that enters the woodland which divides the village of Pannal from Burn Bridge. The path ascends steeply to an obvious track which follows a contour to the right. The wooded hill continues on your left and there is a line of houses on the right at first and then the village football field called Crimple Meadows. At the fence at the end of this path is a stile. Climb this and turn left to follow a delightful footpath which winds its way to Spring Lane. Part of the way along this, ignore the enticing path off the left, and continue with Clark Beck on your right. Upon reaching Spring Lane, cross over the road and turn right to join a path which runs parallel to the road. At the top of the hill there is an old iron gate right, and a stile left. Climb the stile and pass over a small hillock dropping down the other side to a stile into Church Lane. Turn left towards Rossett Green, passing Sandy Bank on the right. Go up the road, and at the entrance of All Saints Court turn right, leaving the road and entering the drive way to a group of several houses.

5. The path ahead goes slightly right, through a wicket gate, and on a contour with spectacular views over the Crimple Valley to Follifoot Ridge. The path then drops down to cross a bridge over Stone Rings Beck. At the top of the hill on the other side of the beck, ignore the stile on the left, and continue to Leeds Road.

6. Cross Leeds Road and walk along Fulwith Mill Lane, and at the junction turn left to return via Hookstone Wood to Hookstone Road. There are several routes through Hookstone Wood offering options which could avoid too much retracing of ground, all leading to a corner close to Hookstone Road.

Short Walk 3
Crimple - Follifoot

Distance: **6.5 miles**   *Map:* **OS Explorer 297 or 289**

Description: **Excellent walking conditions, but wear boots. Very varied, generally level and interesting.**

Pubs: The Travellers Rest, Crimple; The Harewood Arms and the Radcliffe Arms, Follifoot.

Starting Point: **SE 318545**
Hookstone Road on the south side of Harrogate. Off-street parking is possible on St Helen's Road or any of the other roads that lead off Hookstone Road. There is a regular bus service to this point from Harrogate Bus Station, and a train service from Harrogate Station to Hornbeam Park.

Boundary Notes: The Boundary in this area follows the River Crimple.

1. Take the narrow, sign-posted footpath that leads between houses into Hookstone Wood. The path opens out into the wood in under 30 yards and continues straight ahead until reaching Hookstone Wood Ponds. There are boulders and fallen tree branches to indicate the path. At the ponds turn right, pass the wired boundary of the playing fields of St John Fisher School on the right and the edge of a disused quarry, now utilised by enterprising children who have created an amazing adventure cycle park on the left. Turn left on a track that in 25 yards bears right. This lovely woodland ends at a gate. Through this follow the obvious track across the field to a stone bridge which goes over Hornbeam (a.k.a. Hookstone) Beck. After the bridge, the track goes up a small grassy field and to a small gate

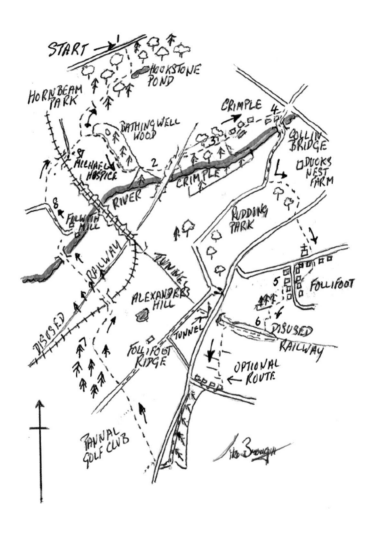

Short Walk 3
Crimple - Follifoot

into a footpath. Ignore the turn to the right (which goes to Crimple House, see Walk 2) and take the stile to the left. Go past a wonderful group of huge beech trees and follow the path down the side of Bathing Well Wood.

Watch out at the beginning of the wood for the old bathing well off to the left of the path at the top of the hill. Although it has been partially filled in for safety, it is an early reminder of Harrogate Spa.

2. Where the path reaches the River Crimple at the bottom of the hill, bear left and exit the wood. Keep along the side of the river and head for the path that goes under the far end of the now disused Old Crimple Viaduct. The path, which is sign-posted, climbs steeply to go under the last arch and on into Crimple woods.

The River Crimple is the boundary of Knaresborough Forest, and the place where the river, the old railway and the bottom of Bathing Well Wood meet, is Mill Hill, the site of an ancient iron smelting mill. Slag and other materials associated with smelting have been found here. Ore was brought here from the Blubberhouses Moor area of the forest along the Iron Gate Road (now Penny Pot Lane).

3. The path through Crimple Wood leads to a stile and into a field with an obvious footpath, and then goes to a stile and enters Crimple Lane. Walk along the lane through the hamlet of Crimple, past the Travellers Rest pub, with views right to Rudding Park.

Rudding Park, now one of the district's outstanding restaurants, was formerly the seat of the Ratcliffe family. Sir Joseph Ratcliffe discovered an ancient Saxon carved stone while work was being done on the chapel in the grounds, and his son Capt. Everard Ratcliffe had it built into the village cross at the head of Follifoot village, in memory of his parents, where it stands to this day.

4. At the end of Crimple Lane, turn right onto the unclassified road over Collin Bridge towards Rudding. Follow the road up the hill and where it turns right at Rudding Park wall, turn left and follow the park wall to the slope, to the left of a pair of big blue gates, that leads up to the Harrogate bypass (A658). Go across this busy road and over the stile ahead, and then straight ahead to the Follifoot road near the church. Turn right, and almost immediately left, through a narrow grassy area to enter a field behind the Harewood Arms Pub. Go diagonally to a stile which leads into the pub car park.

5. On the opposite side of the road to the pub, there is a footpath which twists its way between cottages to a back lane. Go straight ahead and after 50 yards turn left on a broad grassy lane that runs parallel to the main village street. At the bottom of this there is a gate to the right and the path leads on past Horse Pond Beck and wood (recently felled). At the end of the wood the path goes left, then right and left again, then straight on to join the old track bed of the railway. Go through a gate on the right and follow the disused railway track bed to the right. The old railway cutting has been planted with young trees. After just under half a mile the footpath becomes narrower and soon reaches a distinct right turn and goes down a slope. Here there is a choice of two routes.

Boundary Stone 5

6. Option 1. At the bottom of the slope the path enters a tunnel which goes under the Harrogate bypass. Emerge at the other side into a short lane to come out onto the road from Follifoot to Pannal. Turn left and continue along the road past Follifoot Ridge, and in half a mile, at the top of the hill, turn right at a footpath sign into a green lane.

Option 2. Before the tunnel under the by-pass, there is a path to the left that crosses two fields to reach Haggs Lane. At the junction of this with the bypass there is the disused Follifoot to Kirkby Overblow road. Turn left to follow this to where this joins the bypass again, and then cross over the bypass to follow a sign-posted footpath past a part of Pannal golf course. This comes out onto Follifoot Ridge directly opposite the green lane at the end of Option 1.

Just behind Follifoot Ridge is a small pond called Alexander's Hill. This was in fact once a hill, probably the burial place of the victims of a long forgotten battle. Alexander was probably the King of Scotland.

7. In a few yards the green lane enters woodland. Cross through the wood on a muddy path and exit at a footpath gate. Turn right along a well-trodden path to a bridge over the railway line. Go straight ahead here and through a piece of rough ground, which was the route of a now disused railway that went directly to Starbeck. The path ahead takes you over the Crimple on a substantial wood bridge, which is a replacement for one that was washed away in the 2007 floods. Continue up the farm track to a hedge and turn right to join the lower end of Fulwith Mill Lane.

The small mill building to the right here is a very old Forest mill and the few nearby cottages are all that remains of one of the Knaresborough Forest Townships. There is still the dried-up course of the old mill race on the other side of the hedge.

8. Go up the hill and at the top where Fulwith Mill Lane bears left, go right (straight ahead). Bear right at the top towards a bridge over the railway, and soon after this turn left, and then right towards Bathing Well Wood. Watch out for the small gate to the left, which you came through on the outward way, and from this return to Hookstone Wood.

Castley - Huby

Distance: **5.5 miles**   *Map:* **OS Explorer 297**

Description: Easy field and wood walking, with a short crag section (optional).

Pub: The Square and Compass, North Rigton (slightly off route).

Starting Point: **SE 262460**

Drive along Castley Lane which leaves the A658 just before the bridge over the Wharfe at Pool, to the point where the drive of Ings Farm meets Castley Lane. There is a convenient place to park close by at the side of the river.

Boundary Notes: The Boundary in this area follows the River Wharfe. Stone 7 can be seen at the start of the Walk.

1. Before beginning the walk, notice Stone 7, only just visible at the foot of a large tree, at the road side and just opposite the drive of Ings Farm. Walk up the drive towards Ings Farm, and as you approach the farm yard take the path ahead between the cow sheds and the silage store. Go up a short slope to a way-marked gate in the corner. Go through this and up the field with the hedge on your left to a wooden stile. Continue straight ahead, and close to a shelter for farm machinery go through the metal gate on your left, then turn right on a farm drive to the main A658. Cross the busy road and follow it to the left for a third of a mile to enter the drive of Riffa Manor.

2. Walk straight up the drive, and at the gates where it turns right to the house, turn left and pass two cottages. Ahead now a gate can be seen with a yellow way-marker. Go through this and follow a distinct path through

Riffa Wood. After half a mile the path bears right and leaves the wood by a stile, or you can continue another two hundred yards to where it enters the same field by a small gate. Turn left, and keeping the wood on the left, continue to a gate. Leaving the edge of the wood behind, continue across the middle of the field to a field gate and stile. Go over the stile, and continue with a hedge on your right hand until you reach a metal gate on your right where there is a line of thorn trees (an overgrown hedge). Turn right here and through the gate and then follow the hedge and wire fence to reach a wooden gate. Don't go through the gate, but instead turn left and then right through a gap in the stone wall.

3. The path now goes to the right past Bogridge Farm and through a gate onto the drive. Follow the drive left for only a short distance and leave it where it turns sharply right, going straight ahead towards a wood called Bailey's Whins. Go round the wood with it to your left, and, at the top of the short steep field, go through a gate (still with the wood on your left) and follow the edge of the field all the way round until you reach Lower Bank Farm. There is a small iron gate in the corner of the field close by the farm which leads onto the farm road. Turn left along this to reach the public road, Merry Bank Lane.

4. Turn left, and follow this for about half a mile towards Alms Cliff Crag. There are two options here. The easy one is to turn right onto Crag Lane which goes towards North Rigton. The alternative, which is a little more strenuous, is to go straight ahead, and then take the footpath on the right up to the Crag. From the Crag make your way down towards Crag Farm to a stile and then a narrow fenced footpath. This comes out onto Crag Lane directly opposite Crag Farm, so joining the first option. Go along the lane until you reach the yellow gate of Cliff House. Go through the small gate

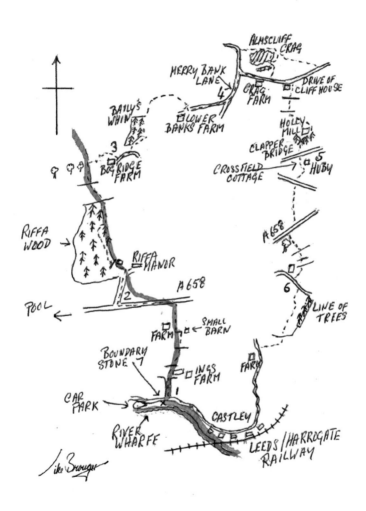

ALMSCLIFF CRAG

MERRY BANK LANE
4
CRAG FARM
DRIVE OF CLIFF HOUSE

BAILY'S WHIN
LOWER BANKS FARM
3
BANK RIDGE FARM

HOLLY MILL BARN

CLAPPER BRIDGE
CROSSFIELD COTTAGE
7
5
HUBY

RIFFA WOOD

RIFFA MANOR

A 658

POOL ←
2

A 658
6
LINE OF TREES

SMALL BARN
FARM

BOUNDARY STONE
7

FARM

INGS FARM

CAR PARK →
1

RIVER WHARFE
CASTLEY
LEEDS / HARROGATE RAILWAY

Mike Brough

Short Walk 4
Castley - Huby

Boundary Stone 7

and into a concreted drive. At the bottom of this go over a stile where a finger-post directs you diagonally right to a metal stile. Go over this and keep the hedge on your left to a stile in the field corner. Cross this, and turning half-right, continue to a gate. Turn half-left here and ahead there is a gate with a stile which follows down the side of a wood to another gate, alongside Holly Hill. The path has been diverted here and a stile on your left leads to a permissive right of way down a field parallel to the original way. There is now a quick succession of three stiles leading to a field path, which avoids the nearby house drive. Half way down the field there is a stile which crosses the drive and leads into a small wood. Follow this gradually round to the right and, keeping to the obvious way, drop down the hill to a kissing gate and clapper bridge. The route then goes straight up the side of the field and through a close to reach the road, which takes local traffic for the village of Huby.

5. Go directly across the road, and then along the drive of Crossfields Cottage. Pass the Cottage and take a narrow little footpath that goes between the garden and the hedge. At a stone building where a green footpath sign points left, turn right and over a stone stile in the corner to continue to another local traffic road. Cross the road and enter another narrow footpath which eventually opens out into a large sloping field. Go straight ahead down the field to a substantial stone step-stile onto the Pool road (A658) close to the bridge over Running Beck. Go right towards Pool for 100 yards looking out for a green footpath sign on the opposite side of the road, partially hidden by an overgrown ash tree. Cross the road and go over the double stile to follow the hedge up the field to a gate. Go through this and continue on the same line to another stile higher up. Still following the same line across the next field, reach another stile that takes you into a deserted piece of land with brambles. There is an easy way through the brambles, and at the far side, notice a yellow way-marker on the other side of a ruined barn on an electricity pole, directing you past Manor Farm to a gate out onto Wescoe Hill Road.

6. Turn left and in 10 yards enter the field opposite at a footpath finger post. Cross the field diagonally left towards a line of conifer trees to reach a stile near the right hand end of the trees. Go over this and follow a well-established hedge round to the right to a gate out onto Castley Lane. Turn left and follow this very quiet road through the village, and then along the side of the River Wharfe back to the car park near Ings Farm.

Short Walk 5
Swinsty - Timble

Distance: **5 miles**   *Map:* **OS Explorer 297**

Description: ***Easy walking, but a tricky beck crossing where a footbridge has been washed away.***

Pubs: The Timble Inn, Timble (check opening times and book your table).

Starting Point: **SE 198536**

The public car park on the eastern side of Swinsty Reservoir.

Boundary Notes: The Boundary in this area follows the Washburn and then turns upstream along the Timble.

The Mystery of the Missing Stile: Before embarking on this walk please read the whole of the description section 1, in case you choose to be slightly boring and not to go in search of missing stiles!

1. Leave the car park and turn right to cross a small spur of the reservoir taking the road (Smithson Lane) and after crossing the causeway, rejoin the reservoir perimeter path. The path joins a lane leading to the dam and to Swinsty Cottage. Cross the dam and take the stile on the left to ascend footpath steps ahead. At the top of the steps and hidden by a large beech tree go over the stone stile, and turn left. Keep the wall on your left until after 50 yards it bears away left, and then bear right on an obvious contour to head for a line of hawthorn trees. Keeping these on your left, climb a stile by a gate and continue straight ahead to another stile. On the other side of this there is a small dike crossed by a wooden bridge. Go straight ahead to the next stile keeping the buildings of Brides Cross Farm on your

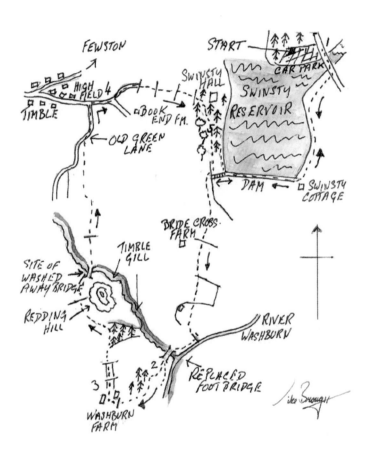

FEWSTON

START

PATH

CAR PARK

SWINSTY HALL

HIGH FIELD 4

TIMBLE

BOOK END FM.

SWINSTY RESERVOIR

OLD GREEN LANE

DAM

SWINSTY COTTAGE

BRIDE CROSS FARM

TIMBLE GILL

SITE OF WASHED AWAY BRIDGE

REDDING HILL

RIVER WASHBURN

REPLACED FOOT BRIDGE

3

2

WASHBURN FARM

Mike Brough

Short Walk 5
Swinsty - Timble

right. Climb this stile and go over another small bridge and follow the dry stone wall on your right, which becomes a line of overgrown hawthorn hedge, to a field gate. Continue to an existing gap, over a ditch and on past an animal shelter on your right. Ignore the gate facing you on the right, and instead, keeping the field boundary on your right, continue down the hill to the corner of the field. There has been a stile in the corner here which has now disappeared, so follow the dry stone wall down to a wooden fence. I cannot possibly recommend climbing this, which would allow you to reach a stile at the side of the Washburn Beck. However, by returning to the top of Swinsty Dam a slightly boring permissive path can be followed to the stile at the side of the Washburn Beck. Ignore the substantial bridge over the Washburn Beck, and instead climb the stile and follow the path keeping the river on your left to a new wooden footbridge over Timble Gill.

Until the 2007 flood there was a delightful miniature arched pack horse bridge here, built by the Ramblers Association, and called the Arthur Adamson Memorial in remembrance of a respected member.

2.   Once over the stream take the path that climbs a short steep embankment and bears right to head for a dry stone wall. Upon reaching this, turn right and make for an ancient and stunted oak tree bearing a yellow way-marker. Turn left here and along the bottom of an old wood, and then up the hill to another dry stone wall also with a yellow way-marker. Continue up the hill with a tiny brook to your left and, keeping the farm buildings on your left, cross a small field to a stile and into the farm yard of Washburn Farm.

3. Turn right in the farm yard and soon the path takes you into a walled farm track, through a gate and then down hill in a field to the corner of a

Timble

small wood. Cross over a tributary of Timble Beck and follow a green track which veers left, and in a short distance climb a stile by a field gate to continue ahead. Over the stile the path passes a few trees and over some stones to a clear path on a level terrace, which follows the contour of Redding Hill to a field gate. Go through the gate and turn right. Climb the short hill with a wall on the right and then go down to a point where there was a foot bridge over Timble Gill before 2007. Cross the beck with great care, and then take the way-marked path which, after three more fields, joins an ancient walled green track to the hill top village of Timble.

Timble and its neighbouring township of Fewston were in 1622 the scene of a very serious witch hunt, when a group of seven local women were charged with devil worship by a local land owner called Thomas Fairfax. The accused were tried at York and, luckily for them, acquitted as they would have been executed if the verdict had been otherwise. Thomas Fairfax was later a general in Oliver Cromwell's

Army during the Parliamentary Civil War and lived at Scow Hall,
according to David Alred in his excellent book 'Washburn Valley
Yesterday'.

4. If you are in need of refreshment, turn left to reach the Timble Inn,
which has recently been reopened. Otherwise, to continue the walk turn
right, and in only 25 yards fork left just before Book End Farm onto a
narrow old green lane. At the end of this lane enter a field through a gate
and continue ahead but slightly left to the next gate. Cross this field
bearing slightly left to another gate in the far left corner. Go through this
and then go straight to a double gate leading into Swinsty Wood. Still
straight ahead brings you to the perimeter wall of Swinsty Hall.

Hidden in the trees is Swinsty Hall, a large house with many chimneys
and gables, tucked away in woodland on its own. The story went that
there was once a simple weaver called Robinson who lived in a tiny
hovel in a hollow close to and on the north side of the village of Timble.
He set off to London to try to better himself and arrived at the height of
the plague. Finding huge sums of money, gold and silver, with no one
left to claim them, he loaded up a cart and returned to his hovel where
he found that the local people, frightened that he might infect them with
the plague, kept well clear. He remained living in his hovel for a year
and carefully washed his gold in a spring known locally as the Green
Well. At the end of a year he was able to have his new house built,
Swinsty Hall, and use his wealth because he was no longer seen as a
threat. Within the Hall is a hollow stone in which coins were placed in
ale during the plague. Although it is now established that this story is
no more than a colourful tale, there was indeed a man called Robinson

who, it is said, foreclosed on a mortgage and acquired the Hall. Perhaps
legend and fact have been mixed in the ensuing years.

5. Turn right (way-marked) through the woods to a flight of four steps and
turn right onto a woodland walled path. After the path widens, continue to
a fence with two stiles. Climb the left-hand one and turn left to descend
the long flight of steps to the reservoir dam. Cross this and return to the car
park via the perimeter path.

Dob Park Pack Horse Bridge.

Dob Park - Folly Hall

Distance: **3.5 miles**   *Map:* **OS Explorer 297**

Description: *This is a particularly short walk, but particularly lovely, with its woods and views.*

Pubs: The Timble Inn, Timble (off route; check opening times and book your table)

Starting Point: **SE198510.**

By car, take the A59 from Harrogate towards Skipton, and turn left onto the B6451 to Otley. Pass the hamlet of Bland Hill and climb to a crest of the hill close to the large radio mast on Norwood Edge. Drop down the hill towards Lindley Reservoir and turn right onto an unclassified road sign-posted to Dob Park. Take a left turn at a distinctive junction just before the road begins to climb Hanging Bank. There are one or two places to park in this vicinity.

Boundary Notes: The Boundary in this area follows first the River Washburn, and then Timble Gill Beck upstream.

---

1.   Walk down the lane towards Dob Park Bridge. The road soon deteriorates into a rough track before reaching an ancient pack horse bridge which arches gracefully over the River Washburn. Cross the bridge and turn right onto a sign-posted footpath. Where the track bears left away from the river side, follow it through a gate/stile. The pile of moss-covered stones is all that remains of Dob Park corn mill. Note the old trough and through the gate stile ahead note the remains of the old mill race. The river at this point meanders a little further away to the right, but as the path

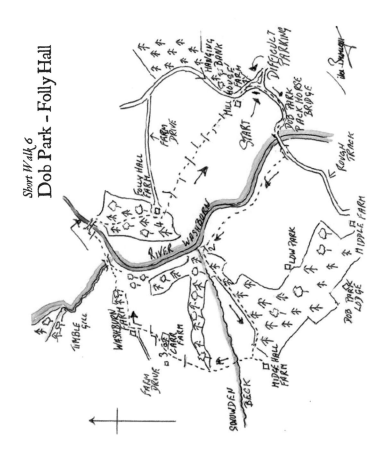

Dob Park Lodge

ahead once more meets the river there is a metal gate-stile on the left. Take this, and continue up a slight hill still with the river to your right, then through another gate/stile to reach a small gate into a wood.

> *The ruins of Dob Park Lodge are just visible above the tree line to your left at this point. It was once the property of a great land-owning family called Vavaseur, and was burnt down about four hundred years ago. It is actually just outside the boundary of Knaresborough Forest, the boundary here being the river Washburn.*

2. Go through the gate and over a tributary of Snowden Beck. On the other side of the beck there is a gate and stile to your left. Enter this and follow the path through the wood, taking the path slightly right, ignoring the arrow way-marker pointing left on the tree. Continue up through the

wood, with Snowden Beck to your right, over two stiles until your reach a narrow green track. Follow this to a T-junction and turn right. (The left path goes to Midge Hall Farm.)

Midge Hall was once owned by the Dibb family, who have also farmed at Folly Hall on the other side of the valley. Folly Hall, an imposing farm house was built in the mid 18th century , stands elegant and tall on a high plateau with a spectacular view down the Washburn valley.

The path goes over Snowden Beck, and in a few yards you are faced with a gate bearing the word 'footpath'. Do not go through this (the word 'no' has worn off!) Bear slightly right, and through a metal gate into a rarely used green lane. Pass a romantic group of ruined farm buildings on your right and then go over a stile into a field. Aim for a stile ahead, to the left of the point of a line of woodland. Go over this and make for another ladder-stile to the left of Carr Farm. Go through a number of animal pens and into the lane that leads to the farm. Cross the lane and go over a stile into a field.

3. From this stile go towards the end of a dry-stone wall, and then, keeping the wall to your left, reach a stile in the corner of the field. (At the time of writing there was a huge branch which had been blown off an ash tree close to the stone stile.) Go straight ahead from here, to enter the farmyard of Washburn Farm. Do not take the obvious track to the right, but instead go left, and then down the farm drive to the right, past a small water system on your left. This was until recently a ford, but has now been piped underground. The farmhouse is now to your left, and at this point turn right, past a line of old stables, to a stile in a stone wall. Go over the stile and, with farm buildings and a small beck to your right, drop down the

slope and down the side of a wood of large trees. At the bottom of the wood go left towards a stunted old tree and then head diagonally towards a yellow arrow nailed to a tree by the river Washburn. There is a path that turns sharp right to follow the river downstream, but don't take this, and instead keep left to drop down a steep slope following the river upstream. Cross the recently renewed foot bridge, and continue upstream to a stile, and upon reaching a farm road turn right over a farm bridge. The track now climbs up through woodland to Folly Hall Farm.

The recently renewed foot bridge replaces a delightful narrow arched stone bridge that was built by the Ramblers Association many years ago and called the Arthur Adamson Bridge. Although very well built, it was unable to survive the might of the 2007 floods which swept away so many bridges in the area.

4. As you enter the farmyard, keep right and follow the way round with the farm house to your left and then go straight ahead through a gate into a field. The way ahead, easily identified along the side of the wall by higher ground, has been a lane in the past and is now the right of way. The route goes through five fields before joining the Dob Park Road at the foot of Hanging Bank. Continue now the short distance to the top of the lane at which the walk started.

The Washburn valley has been home and work place for many families for many generations and is remarkable because to this day there are a lot of names that remain the same. This walk passes through the farms of such families: Washburn Farm of the Addymans, and Midge Hall and Folly Hall of the Dibbs.

John o' Gaunt's Castle

Distance: **3.5 or 4.5 miles**   *Map:* **OS Explorer 297**

Description: *A very short but interesting walk, although it can be very muddy in winter. Welly boots recommended.*

Pub: The Sun Inn, Norwood (slightly off route.)

Starting Point: **SE 215552**

The small parking place (three to four cars) at the left-hand side of Penny Pot Lane, to the west of Harrogate, just past Willow House.

Boundary Notes: This walk is well within the Forest, in the old area of Haverah Park.

1. From the parking place, do not take the footpath sign-posted 'Restricted Byway', but follow the far less inviting Penny Pot Lane for a quarter of a mile west to take the farm drive sign-posted to Trees Farm. Walk down the drive and, where it veers left to the farm, go straight ahead to pass Trees House and through a small gate into a narrow footpath. The path crosses a rickety stile and passes a wet and muddy area of bracken, where at some time in the distant past there was a stone causeway to make the going better. The view up onto Blubberhouses Moor is excellent here on a good sunny day. The path drops down a hill to join the drive of Bank End Farm. Turn left on this and pass the farm to your left to go through a gate and stile to your right.

2. In a few yards there is a stile on your right marked the 'Dales Way'. Climb this and continue ahead to a small metal gate, and then on to a large metal gate. Another small metal gate ahead is combined with a wooden

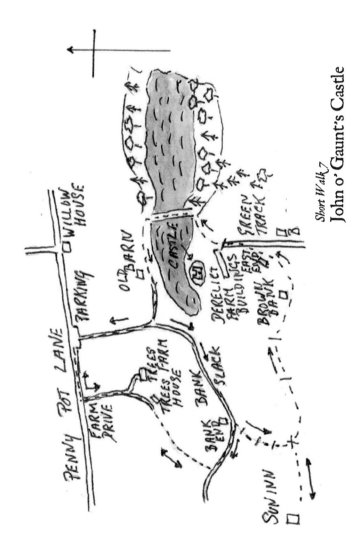

Short Walk 7
John o' Gaunt's Castle

bridge over a small stream. Go over this and pass through a large field with no distinct path but a thriving crop of reeds and rushes towards a kissing gate visible in the corner of a wall ahead. If refreshment is required this gate leads to the Sun Inn.

3. Alternatively, continue up the hill keeping the dry stone wall on your right. There are a couple of now defunct stiles and two to climb. Negotiate the second with care as it has a steep descent. The field ahead is very rough with rushes and reeds, and quite muddy underfoot. The best way is probably to go straight up the hill after the tricky stile and, towards the top, veer right to reach the farm yard of Brown Bank Farm. Pass the end of the farm buildings and turn left to go past the front of the farm house. You will now be faced by two field gates. Take the right-hand one, which has path arrows on it, and continue straight ahead keeping the wall to your left. Keep going through a stile to reach a second stile identified by a substantial yellow-painted wooden post.

4. Crossing this, you will see another similar post diagonally across the next field. There is a magnificent old manor house called East End before you now, with a gate and ladder stile. Go through this and continue straight ahead to a point where the path bends slightly left. Keep to the right at a water course and make for an un-gated opening in the wall to your right, which leads into an old green track. Follow this left to an iron gate and the ruins of John o' Gaunt's Castle.

This is actually an ancient hunting lodge, probably predating John o'
Gaunt. It may well have been built in the time of Edward III, as the
area you are now in was then an enclosure within the Forest of

Knaresborough. There was a similar enclosure at Bilton. The reservoir below is part of the old Claro Water Scheme, as is the nearby Beaver Dyke Reservoir.

5. After enjoying the castle and the view over the water, return to the path that passes the derelict farm buildings and go down an old sunken track to the dam between the reservoirs. At the other side, turn left on an obvious track to pass a group of quite picturesque but sadly derelict farm buildings, and continue over a small stream to a footpath 'T' junction. Here there are two options. Turn right for the 3.5 mile version of the walk. The track is charming and winds its way back to where you left your car, and no one will blame you.

6. The other option is to turn left for further adventure. Within only a few yards the path goes slightly to the right and follows for quite a distance a kind of hollowed-out green track.

This is called 'Bank Slack', and it makes John o' Gaunt's Castle seem positively modern! It is part of an extensive defence system built by the Brigante Tribe in their ongoing battle with the invading Romans. Although the track holds water and can be wet, it is worth the extra walk just to savour 2000 years of history.

7. Bank Slack leads to Bank End Farm where you can return by the paths past Trees House and Trees Farm taken on the outward route. This will come to approximately 4.5 miles.

Short Walk 8
Darley - Cinder Hills

Distance: **4.5 miles**   *Map:* **OS Explorer 298**

Description: ***Easy field and wood walking.***

Pub: The Wellington Inn, Darley. *Refreshments:* Darley Mill

Starting Point: **SE 211593**

Parking place for three or four cars at the side of the road through Darley village, close to the junction with Stumps Lane (B6165). There is a regular bus service through Nidderdale and a bus stop at the bottom of Stumps Lane.

Boundary Notes: The Boundary in this area runs along the River Nidd, before turning up Darley Beck. Stones 31, 32 and 33 can be visited by a short detour on this Walk. Stones 35, 36 and 38 can also be reached, but require permission as they are on private land.

1. Walk in an easterly direction along the road towards Birstwith for a quarter of a mile, past the drive to Moke Hill Farm, and then turn right into a green lane. Walk up the lane, with a deep tree-lined ditch on your left, for half a mile to reach the beginning of a narrow metalled road and the small hamlet of Springfield. Turn sharp left, and go through a gate onto a rough lane, and past a number of old partially ruined buildings, to what has been a tiny ford.

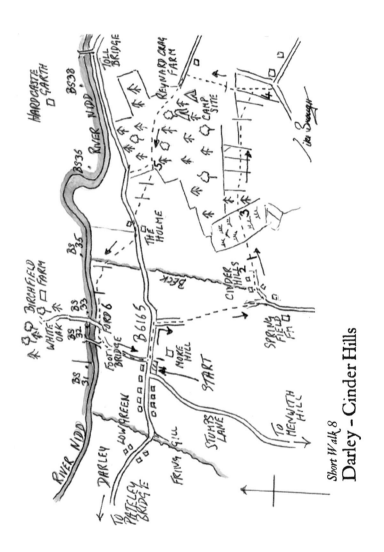

The group of buildings is all that remains of what is believed to be a medieval 'smelt mill and bloomery' known as Cinder Hills. It is worth pausing a while here to identify the foundations of old buildings and a simple water system that might once have been seen as advanced technology.

2. Continue over a stile ahead, and then turn right past a dilapidated and tumble-down old cottage constructed of timber and asbestos. Continue past another old stone building which was almost certainly part of the 'heavy industry' foundry described above. Cross the field to a clearly visible stone stile. On the other side of the stile, continue in the same line to a stile which takes you into an area of rough moorland. Still in the same direction, pass a line of three small silver birch saplings and cross another stile into the wood ahead.

3. The path goes slightly to the right through the wood and after leaving it, goes on to the top of a small paddock. In a short distance reach a plot of land that appears to be a building site. Keep left, with a wire fence to your left, and then go right directly across the site to a small gate (which may be hidden by machinery), and then continue straight ahead through five fields, all with stiles or gates.

4. At the fifth of these fields, the path goes diagonally right to an obvious gap in the wall. Go through the gap and then climb the stile ahead. The path goes diagonally right here, to the far corner at Back Lane, but do not head for this. Instead, turn left and follow the wall to reach a gate on your left. Reaching the corner, turn sharp left and go through the gate, then immediately turn right. This path, which is broad to start with, passes a

recently planted wood and becomes a pleasant twisty path through a mossy and gorsey area with mature woodland to the left. It reaches a narrow lane and here you turn left. The road comes to a dead end at the entrance of a camp site at Reynards Crag, but there is a sign-posted footpath to the right of the camp site gate. The path ahead is tree-lined and green, and as it becomes proper woodland it is paved with ancient stone slabs worn by generations of feet. The path passes a lovely old pond. Keep a lookout for woodpeckers!

5. The obvious path veers slightly right and the road ahead comes into view. Bear left here (way-marked) to a stile in the corner of the wood, and walk across four fields to converge with the same road that you started out on, but a little farther from Darley. Cross the road and walk along it towards Darley for 200 yards past the Holme, and go over a stile to the right. The path crosses this field diagonally to the far left corner and then goes through into the next field, before going down to a path along the river side.

There was a very flourishing laundry in the building behind the Holme until the mid 20th century.

6. In a short distance the riverside path reaches a place on the Nidd known as Haxby Hippings, an old name for this ford.

Nearby is a foot bridge, and it is worth crossing this as there are a number of Boundary Stones which I have marked with their numbers on the map of this Walk. To see Stone 31, take the path to the left, which comes to a dead end at a wall, where the stone can be seen on the other side. Retrace your steps back to the bridge, keep straight ahead

Boundary Stone 31

*and in a few yards you will see Stone 32, on the right between the
footpath and the river. Both Boundary Stones 31 and 32 have only
their tops visible above the ground, with only their numbers visible,
probably due to the build-up of silt carried down the river in times of
flood. In a few more yards the old track leading from Haxsby Hippings
comes into view. Here our path veers left to join the old track at a point
where it is possible to cross it and continue along the river side. Across
the track, and still by the river, is Boundary Stone 33, standing proud
with all of its markings visible. This stone had been washed out of its
footings and into the Nidd, and was found and re-erected by John
Webster and Cyril Mason supported by a Historical Society about 20
years ago. Stones 31, 32, and 33 can be seen without going onto
private land. Boundary Stone 34 formerly stood 50 yards further along
the river side, but is now missing, and in another 50 yards stands
Boundary Stone 35, but it is private land and permission to visit must*

*be gained from Mr M. Smith at HACS Ltd., the Old Station, Ripley,
Harrogate. Stones 36 and 38 are also on private land, and permission
must be sought from: Mrs H Patrick, Flo's Farm, Hartwith,
Summerbridge, Harrogate. Near to Stones 36 and 38 and a little
further back from the river is one of the fine old farm houses of
Nidderdale, Hardcastle Garth, named after a family who originally
built it.*

7. From the south side of the foot bridge follow the track through the old disused railway embankment and through a metal gate. Now walk up the track to rejoin the road into the village of Darley at the place where the walk started.

*At the junction with Stumps Lane, the murder took place in August
1850 of Mary Ann Skaife by her boyfriend James Atkinson after a
lovers' tiff. James Atkinson escaped the gallows on the grounds of
insanity. The girl's grave is at Hartwith, and has the epitaph:*

> *" The victim of the murderer's blade,*
> *Beneath a gory course was laid,*
> *Her soul we trust, to realms has flown,*
> *Where theft and murder are unknown."*

*There used to be a memorial stone at the place where there is now the
village boundary stone of Darley.*

8. This is a short walk, and for those who may choose to extend it by about a mile and a half. Instead of taking the track back to the village from the footbridge at Haxby Hippings, go through a small gate close to the bridge and follow the river Nidd upstream. The field path is level and easy going. The embankment of the now disused Nidd Valley Railway is to your left,

and the Nidd to your right. Ignore the old bridges that pass through the railway embankment, and reach the confluence of Darley Beck with the Nidd. Turn left here, ignoring the inviting little footbridge over Darley Beck, and keeping the beck to your right pass over the old railway embankment. Continue with the beck on your right, to reach another small footbridge over the beck. There is a path directly up the field to the left that leads to Stocks Green in the centre of the village. If on the other hand you have decided to avail yourself of the excellent fare at either Darley Mill or the Wellington Inn, then cross the footbridge and turn left past Low Hurst Farm and onto the main B6451 road. Replete, the best way back to the car is simply through the village.

While in Darley, you may find it interesting to take a look at the memorial hall in the centre of the village. The building was at one time the dining-hall for the navvies at Scar House when the Bradford reservoirs were being built, and was rescued and transported here. There is, and always has been, a very active community at Darley, and there are often plays and dances at the hall.

Short Walk 9
Darley - Thornthwaite

Distance: **7.5 miles**   *Map:* **OS Explorer 298**

*Description: **Easy and charming walk with much interest, wear boots!***

Pub: The Wellington Inn, Darley. *Refreshments:* Darley Mill

Starting Point: **SE 211593**

Parking place for three or four cars at the side of the road through Darley village, close to the junction with Stumps Lane (B 6165). There is a regular bus service through Nidderdale and a bus stop at the bottom of Stumps Lane.

Boundary Notes: The Boundary runs along the River Nidd, before turning up Darley Beck, which becomes Padside Beck.

1. Walk north along the lane opposite to the above parking place, through the disused railway embankment, to the footbridge over the river Nidd. (If you cross the bridge you can see Stones 31, 32 and 33; see Short Walk 8 Section 6.) Take the stile on the left immediately before the footbridge, and walk along the river side. At the point where Darley Beck joins the Nidd, do not cross the small footbridge, but bear left and, keeping the beck to your right, follow it upstream. After passing the remains of the old, now disused Nidd Valley railway embankment, still keeping the beck on your right, reach a small footbridge. Cross this, and where the footpath divides go through the squeeze stile and turn left (the right fork goes to Pyefield House). The going can be very soft across the fields, past Low Hurst Farm. After passing the farm, head for the far left-hand corner of the field, to a

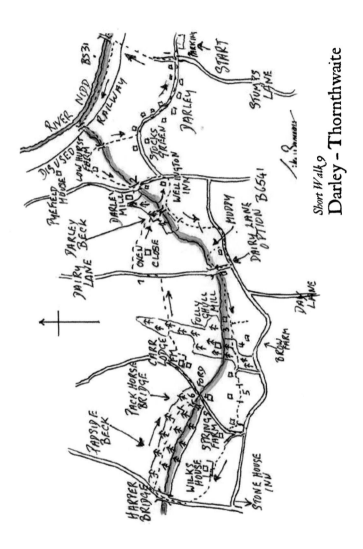

Short Walk 9
Darley - Thornthwaite

Boundary Stone 33

stile which takes you onto the road opposite Darley Mill.

Watch out for the outlet arch of the old Brightwater Mill to your left. This was once a flax mill, later converted to make paint. It finally closed about 50 years ago. There were formerly two other mills in Darley: Fring Gill Mill, which was also a flax mill but later made twine, and is now converted into housing, and Darley Mill, which made linen and which is now largely restored and running as a retail outlet.

2. Now cross the road and walk past Darley Mill, and close to a house go over a stile on your right. Although the ground in these two fields is wet, there is a firm edge along the side of the wall, making the going comfortable. The gates ahead are usually open but there are stiles if not. The path passes a pair of gate posts with neither gate nor wall, and in the field corner ahead passes close by the beck and a wall for a short narrow stretch. This opens out into a field that has a steep slope down to the beck side. Keep on the top side of this slope, following the rim to a stile by a rowan tree. Cross this to an obvious metal gate, and then follow the side of

the wall up to the road from Darley to Thornthwaite. Turn right towards Thornthwaite, and stay on the road for three-quarters of a mile, and then turn right into Dairy Lane. In 50 yards at the bottom of the hill at Folly Gill Bridge, turn left onto a rough lane. There is a gate halfway along with a pedestrian gate at the side. (It is possible to avoid some of the road walking by turning right near to a cottage, and following a public footpath through some lovely woodland to come out at Folly Gill bridge, but it is very muddy indeed, although there are stone slabs which can help a bit).

3. Follow the rough lane past Folly Ghyll Mill and a number of houses and cottages until the lane bears fairly sharply left.

Folly Ghyll Mill was also a flax mill, and was burnt down about 300 years ago. When it was rebuilt it was considered to be the cutting edge of technology, perhaps even too modern!

Take the stile at the corner, and continue up the grassy field towards a group of large beech trees. There is a stone stile among these trees which leads onto the drive of Folly Hall. Go directly over the drive to another stile and into a wood. The obvious path bears left at the top of the wood and through a narrow section. When the wood widens out, keep right to reach a stile that leads onto the drive of a dales house. As the drive turns left here, go straight on (or technically turn right.) Soon there is a stile on the left taking you into a field. Climb this and turn right. In a short distance there is another house drive, which you cross and go over a piece of grassy open ground where the footpath leads to a stile by a line of large conifers. Go over the stile and turn left to follow the diverted route round the house grounds.

Notice as you walk through this section of woodland that there are a number of circular shallow hollows. These are all that remains of medieval coal mines. This poor quality brown coal was called lignite.

4. The path emerges by a stile into the first of four fields. Cross these in a straight line and, at a stile onto a lane close to a farm house, turn left and reach the Thornthwaite road. Turn right here, and in 20 yards bear right on the road sign-posted to Thornthwaite. In another 20 yards bear left onto the farm drive of Springs Farm. Walk through the farmyard, and enter a green lane that leads on towards Wilks House. The path crosses the drive to Wilks House and continues along its boundary wall. Halfway along this wall, there is a stile into the garden, hidden from the house by a high hedge. After entering the garden, keep left and leave it by a stile into a field. Continue, with the wall to your left, and from the next field boundary bear half-right towards a gate out onto the road. Follow the road to the right to Harper Bridge over Padside Beck, and then 25 yards further on take the sign-posted footpath to the right by a stile into the wood. Follow this wood all the way down to the ancient pack-horse bridge at Thornthwaite.

Watch out for the many marked stones and remains of medieval rural industry.

5. Join the road, and go left over the ford and up the hill to the drive of Carr Lodge Farm. Go along the drive and past the farm buildings, turning left at the end of them. Walk up the side of the buildings to a gate, where you can turn right, and after 50 yards go over a stile on the left to cross the field towards the side of the wood, where there is a marker on the wall.

Climb the difficult stile into the wood and go straight ahead to exit the wood at the top of a long straight track leading down to Dairy Lane.

6. Turn left, and then turn right into a field at the first footpath sign. Go straight ahead to another stile, and continue, keeping the field wall on your right. At the bottom of the field the wall veers slightly left, and here watch out for a stile into a small wood. The path is easy to follow to a wooden footbridge across the beck. At the other side turn left and return to the B6451 near to Darley Mill. Cross the road and return by the outward route past Low Hurst Farm to the footbridge. Cross this and turn left, but instead of returning on the same way that you came, take the noticeable path that crosses the field to the right, up to Stocks Green. Now follow the road to the left through Darley Village to the starting point near the bottom of Stumps Lane.

Pack Horse Bridge, Thornthwaite

Padside - Thruscross

Distance: **5 miles**   *Map:* **OS Explorer 298**

Description: A delightful and varied walk with good going underfoot, close up views of Padside Hall and the joy of the walk along the edge of Thruscross Reservoir.

Pubs: The Stonehouse Inn (slightly off route).

Starting Point: **SE 147602**

About half way along the minor road from Blubberhouses to Greenhow, a road, Braithwaite Lane, turns off to the north-east, and passes the drive to Padside Hall. You can park close to the drive, but avoid blocking the field gate.

Boundary Notes: Fall Beck is the Boundary of the Forest, and soon becomes Padside Beck and then Darley Beck before flowing into the Nidd. Stone 29 is at the start of the Walk.

1. Walk north along Braithwaite Lane towards a bridge which crosses Fall Beck, and just before the bridge there is a wall stile on the right. From this, Stone 29 can clearly be seen standing among gorse bushes a few yards west of the beck and about 50 yards away. The path that crossed this field has now been diverted.

2. After viewing Stone 29, return to where you have parked and go along the drive of Padside Hall. A way-marked diverted path turns off the drive left, where a line of huge spruce trees ends at stone gate pillars, and an area of wood begins. It goes down the side of the wood keeping close to the dry

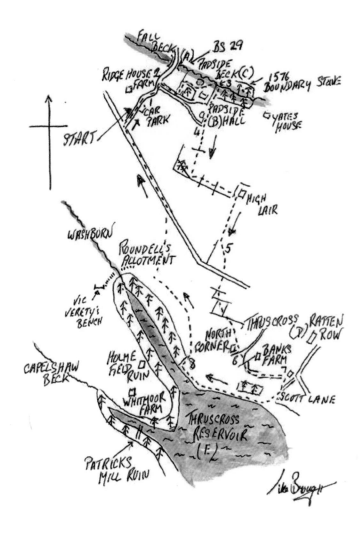

FALL BECK
BS 29
RIDGE HOUSE FARM
PADSIDE BECK (C)
1576 BOUNDARY STONE
CAR PARK
PADSIDE (B) HALL
YATES HOUSE
START
HIGH LAIR
WASHBURN
ROUNDELL'S ALLOTMENT
VIC VERETY'S BENCH
THRUSCROSS RATTEN (D) ROW
NORTH CORNER
BANKS FARM
HOLME FIELD RUIN
CAPELSHAW BECK
WHITMOOR FARM
SCOTT LANE
THRUSCROSS RESERVOIR (E)
PATRICKS MILL RUIN

Short Walk 10
Padside - Thruscross

Boundary Stone 29

stone wall. Climb the wood stile to enter a field at the bottom of the wood. Continue another 20 yards, still with the wall, and turn right past an old tree to pass on the right side of two ponds. The path passes just below the Hall to reach a stile ahead at the bottom of another wood close to the beck side.

Padside Hall is an old peel tower, built by the Ingilbys of Ripley Castle, and one of the oldest houses in Nidderdale. Early residents of the hall were the Wigglesworths who, Alastair Laurence tells us in his book 'West End, A Sunken Village'. For many generations they lived at Padside Hall and held the hereditary title of Lord Constable of the Forest, a title which was discontinued in the early years of the 20th century.

3. Climb the wooden stile and turn to the right, with the fence at the edge of the wood on your right, up the steep hill and, after a dilapidated stile, pass close by the perimeter wall of the Hall.

It is possible to make a short detour here on a public footpath that follows the Forest Boundary, which is the beck, to an interesting Stone which was probably originally erected in the 1576 Perambulation. To do this, cross the beck and in another 30 yards you will see the stone, almost hidden by a fallen tree. You will then have to retrace your footsteps. In the 1770 Perambulation the Boundary is described as follows: "then down the fence to the close of Edward Yates in which there are three bounder stones marked 'F' on the south side for Forest, and 'T' for Ingilby on the north; and then through the house of the said Edward Yates, and by four encroachments taken from Hayshaw Moor to Harrow Gap where the Monk Wall begins". The house is now known as Yates House. Edward Yates was brought before the Leat Court at Knaresborough Castle and fined for encroachment. There are another two similarly marked boundary stones and permission would need to be gained to view them from Mr G Favell at Yates House, Braithwaite, Padside, Harrogate.

4. A few yards past Padside Hall there is a cottage. Turn left onto its drive, and follow this for a short distance up to a sharp bend. Follow the bend right, and climb a stone stile (unmarked) on your left. Walk straight ahead and go between a pair of gate posts and up to a metal gate by a small clump of trees. At the gate, turn left and follow the wall across two fields, until, just before High Lair, turn right through a stile and, after two fields, reach the Greenhow Hill road.

5. Go straight across the road and into a field opposite. Walk straight ahead with the dry stone wall on your left. At the corner of this field, go diagonally left and at the next field diagonally again to a stile which enters a recently planted birch wood. The diagonal line continues through the middle of the wood and on in the same line to reach the tiny hamlet of Thruscross and North Corner Barn (now converted into a private house).

6. Go straight ahead, still on the same line, across a piece of common rough pasture, past a way-marker post to a ladder-stile. On the other side of this, go ahead keeping the wall on your left, and keep following it as it turns gradually left. There are way-markers which direct you to the left of an overgrown hedge, and on past a redundant squeeze-stile.

7. The path reaches the wall of a house with a gate marked 'private'. Turn right here, past an old tree in the garden, and down the field past an electricity pole with a way-marker, to a gate onto the old road across the valley. Where this road (once called Scott Lane) disappears into the dark depths of the reservoir, turn right and keep on with Thruscross Reservoir to your left. Before the reservoir was built, Scott Lane led to the then-deserted village of West End.

There was once an inn in the nearby hamlet of Thruscross called the
'Hanging Gate', which was marked by a small gate hanging in the tree,
and owned by a family called Peel, but that ceased to serve ale about
150 years ago. The Inn was at the side of the road from Thruscross
Dam, in one of the cottages now known as Ratten Row. There is
neither Inn nor hanging gate now, although the old tree with

Patrick's Mill, Thruscross Reservoir

*a tree house in it may be the same. It is said that Mr Alec Simpson, a
more recent landlord, had a notice that read: "This gate hangs well and
hinders none, Refresh and pay and travel on." In Ratten Row there
was a blacksmith called Mr Horsman, and the mould he used for
making cart wheels is still outside. The Abbotts ran the Stone House
Inn a little further up the road, where they sold ginger beer at 1d per
pint to wagon men carrying quick lime from the kilns on Greenhow at
Coldstones. This inn closed a few years ago, but has recently reopened.
There are still members of both the Peel and Abbott families living in
the district.*

*Thruscross was the last of the Washburn reservoirs to be built, and
when it was completed in 1966 its waters flooded the old deserted
village of West End. The valley was particularly lovely and for many*

years visited by numerous people for sight-seeing and weekend picnics. The village, which clustered round its two little bridges and its church, was deserted in the 19th century because its water-powered flax-mills were unable to compete with competition from the south of Yorkshire, where the linen industry had embraced steam power. The cost of bringing coal on toll roads made the finished product too expensive. Many of the villagers moved off to places like Barnsley, where coal was cheaper because of the close proximity of the South Yorkshire coal fields. There were four or five mills in West End, including Aked's Mill, Patrick's Mill and Walker's Mill.

8. Stay by the water until the path moves away from the reservoir at a wood. Go up the side of the wood, on a path with rough steps and over a ladder-stile out onto the open moor. The permissive path is clear with marker-posts, and where it is a bit muddy in winter there are stepping-stones. On the open moor there is a ladder-stile and a post with way-markers.

9. Continue straight ahead here and at a sike which comes in from the right turn to follow it upstream. This moor is called Roundell's Allotment after the Rev. William Roundell who bought this land when the Forest was divided up after the last Perambulation. In half a mile there is a gate that leads out onto the Greenhow Road. Go through this, turn left, and in another half mile go right on to the minor road that leads to the drive to Padside Hall, and the beginning of the walk.

Short Walk *11*
Bilton Park

Distance: **6 miles**   *Map:* **OS Explorer 297 or 298**

Description: Unlike the other walks described in this book, this is a linear walk, but a return can be easily made on public transport. It follows the Nidd downstream, but could easily be done in the reverse direction.

Pubs: The Gardeners Arms, Old Bilton; the Worlds End, High Bridge Knaresborough.

Starting Point: **SE 304555**

The bus station in Harrogate.

Boundary Notes: The Boundary in this area runs along the River Nidd.

1. Walk to the bottom of Station Parade and then down to the bottom of Lower Station Parade. Cross Bower Road and turn right and under the railway bridge. Turn left to pass the Asda Supermarket and on through the car park. Go through the open gateway into the lorry park and straight ahead reach the path that passes under a foot bridge. The path is separated from the railway on the left by a metal fence. The path enters Grove Park Road, and then continue left, still with the railway to the left. The footpath leads to a bridge over the railway designed for pedestrians and bicycles. On the other side of the railway, keep right and follow the old disused rail track for a mile to Bilton Junction and Bilton Lane. There is a small car park here. Turn right on Bilton Lane and just before the Gardeners Arms, go sharp left on a narrow lane. The lane goes over a bridge over Bilton Beck and then uphill to Beck Farm.

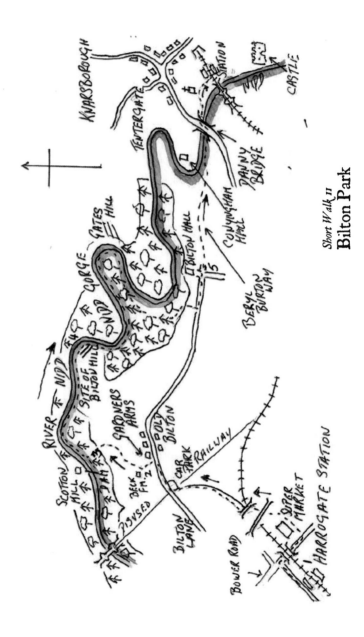

Short Walk 11
Bilton Park

Scotton Mill

2. To the right of the gate to Beck Farm there is a gate into a narrow little footpath, overhung with hedging forming a canopy. The path opens out into a field, and keeping the hedge to your right, proceed until you reach another little path with high hedging on both sides. This leads into a deeply-grooved path on woodland-type steps into the Nidd Gorge. At the T-junction ahead, turn right to continue the walk. However, it is worth going left as a detour for a better view of Scotton Mill and its river dam. Once you have seen it, return to the T-junction.

Scotton Mill was originally a township corn mill, then turned into a flax mill, and finally used as a private electricity generator, belonging to Lord Mountgarret of Nidd Hall. It is now converted into a private residence.

3. Follow the path downstream close to the River Nidd. This is part of the boundary of the forest and also part of the Forest enclosure of Bilton Park. Continue now through this fabulous gorge and wonder at the fact that you are within a mile and a half of two busy towns, in country that is as wild and lovely as any in the land. In less than half a mile the path enters a clearing, although there are plenty of bushes and scrub. Passing through this section, look out for the remains of Bilton Mill. There are still fragments of its walls along the river bank, and its mill dam can still clearly be seen. Among the apparently random humps and bumps in the land there are the remains of the old mill race.

Bilton had an important role to play in Forest life. It was one of the earliest townships of the Forest and it had specific responsibilities. Its community was directly charged with the maintenance of the 'Park Pale', some of which still exists on the land of Bilton Village Farm.

4. Continue along the banks of the Nidd to cross a small streamlet and a stile into more woodland, and follow the path passing a well-built wooden footbridge with stone piers. Do not cross the river, but keep beside it, through an area with some large beech trees where the footpath and river diverge. The path now continues up some woodland steps and through bracken to more steps, and then reaches a high level, where in winter there are fine views of the river on a bend far below. The path comes out at a T-junction, where the way is sign-posted to the left, and the way to the right is barred by a metal gate. The way ahead is clear and comes out onto the Bilton Hall end of Bilton Lane. Go through the gate and left on this lane, and in five hundred yards reach the drive of Bilton Hall.

5. Do not go down the drive, but go straight ahead here onto a footpath known today as the Beryl Burton Way after the girl who was a world champion cyclist and who is rightly regarded as a local heroine.

Bilton Hall, now a residential home, was at one time the seat of a family called Stockdale who played a significant part in local history. They were appointed as Foresters, along with the Slingsby family, and at one time represented Knaresborough in Parliament.

The Beryl Burton Way crosses a cattle grid into a field and follows a hedge to drop down to another cattle grid, which leads into the woodland close to the river again. Continue now to High Bridge at Knaresborough, previously known as Danny Bridge.

The house on the opposite side of the river is Conyngham Hall, and is now a business centre.

The options now are either to take a bus back to Harrogate (there is a stop directly across the road, and buses every seven minutes), or to cross the road, cross the bridge and walk along Waterside, then bear left at the side of a thatched house up Waterbag Bank to the railway station, to catch a train. Either bus or train will return you to Station Parade in Harrogate.

Shaw Mills - Wipley - Hill Top

Distance: **5 miles** *Map:* **OS Explorer 298**

Description: *A slightly hilly walk, but easy and with plenty of interest.*

Pubs: The Boar's Head, Ripley, slightly off route.

Starting Point: **SE 257625**

The centre of Shaw Mills village. Take the Harrogate - Ripon road (A61) and turn left at the second roundabout at Ripley onto the Pateley Bridge road (B6165). After two miles turn right at the cross roads at Burnt Yates Bar to Shaw Mills.

Boundary Notes: The Walk passes Stones 42, 43 and 44.

The name of the Fountains Abbey corn miller was Shaw, and it is from him that the village gets its name.

1. Walk from the bridge over Thornton Beck towards Bishop Thornton, and at the sharp left-hand bend there is a footpath off to the right hidden behind a crash barrier. Take the path over a small stone stile and between hedges to enter a field. The path is marked to go diagonally towards an electricity pole, but if the field is planted with a crop it is easier and less muddy to follow the boundary to the right. Keeping the field fence on your right, continue to a metal gate. Go straight ahead here and at a point where there is a stile off to the right leading to a white-painted foot bridge, ignore it and instead turn left and up the field until in the corner you reach a wooden gate on the right.

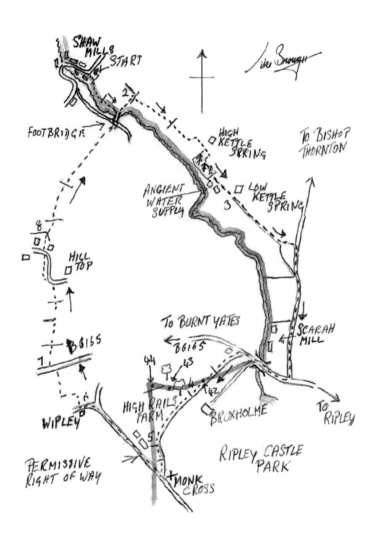

Short Walk 12
Shaw Mills - Wipley - Hilltop

2. Go through this gate (way-marked), and continue straight ahead following a high-level green path, with a wall on your left, past old oaks and hawthorn trees. The path drops down to a small bridge over Cold Beck, then goes through a metal gate and on up the field, until the wall to the left turns away. Follow the wall and the old track, which bears round to the right and up a steep hill, towards High Kettle Spring Farm. Go through the muddy farm yard with the buildings to your left and take the small hunting gate on the right just opposite the farm house to the left. The path drops down through a small wood and past a long-forgotten quarry and on through a small wooden gate.

The buildings on your right are the Ripley village water supply, which was originally set up by Fountains Abbey. The main building is the present supply, and replaces the more dilapidated one. The small 'beehive' structure nearby, from which the water comes, dates back many centuries. The water, which has never been known to dry up, is good, but very hard.

3. Go on to Low Kettle Spring Farm, past the pig units and then along the drive to the Bishop Thornton road at Scarah Bank. Turn right, and when this road joins the B6165 Pateley Bridge road, turn right again. Cross the road and turn right towards Pateley Bridge and in quarter of a mile cross Scarah Bridge, or Godswin Bridge as it was once known, and in about 50 yards take the sign-posted footpath that follows the wall of Ripley Park off to the left.

On the bank of Thornton Beck, below Scarah Bridge, once stood Stone 42, but within the last 20 years this disappeared without trace. I have

Replacement of Boundary Stone 42

been fortunate to obtain a suitable replacement stone due to the generosity of Mr Mark Smith of High Rails Farm and HACS Civil Engineers. He kindly donated a huge former gate post of almost identical proportions to the original, and agreed to erect it at a suitable nearby place. I decided that since the original position was on private land, a better site would be 50 yards or so away, along the side of Ripley Park wall, as more people would be able to see it from the public right of way towards High Rails Farm at Whipley. Mr Andrew Walmsley of Scarah Bank Farm has kindly agreed to permit the new stone to be placed on his land. I have had it inscribed by a stone mason, with 42 at the top, K F below, and under that 2010, as it was thought that to put 1767 would be a deceit, and Stones 8 and 9, which are now marked 1825, had already set a precedent.

4. Continue up the field and then through a gate into the next, to the point where the Park Wall veers off slightly left. At this point go straight ahead and you will see that close by a large oak tree stands Stone 43, and 100 yards farther on and a little to the right, at the other side of a wood and wire fence, stands Stone 44, both of these at a rakish angle

> *There are several large oak trees in this area, and it is likely that they all grew from acorns that had fallen from a huge oak that grew at this spot, known as the Godwin Oak, which is mentioned in both the 1576 and the 1767 Perambulations.*

From the Perambulation of 1576:

> *" and uppe a lytle syke called Black Syke running upon the out side of Ripley Parke payle unto Gaweswane oke"*

From the 1770 Perambulation:

> *"formally a park fence, in which the remains of an old oak tree known by the name of Godwin Oak, where stands the bounder stone marked 43 KF 1767".*

The old name Godwin Bridge (now Scarah Bridge) was also taken from this tree.

5. Return now to the park wall and follow it to two kissing gates. Go through to join the lane that follows the park wall towards Saddlers Barn, but turn right and go through High Rails Farm yard. This lane is a permissive right of way and was at one time known as Dog Lane.

> *At the point where you turn right, the park wall top dips a couple of courses of stones. Look over the wall at this low place and across about 30 yards of tree-felling debris, notice an unusual standing stone. It is thought by some to be the Monk Cross that formerly stood at the upper*

end of Dog Lane near the fork at Whipley, while others think it could be Corpse Cross. There are several theories about it, including the possibility that it could be the burial place of Archil, a Danish thane who ruled a large part of this country about the time of the Norman Conquest. Dark Hall, which is close to the bridle way from Ripley to Clint, at a place on the map called Saddler Carr, is thought to have been Archil's house.

6. In a third of a mile the lane forks; turn left here towards Wipley. There is a small gate on the right of this lane with a footpath straight ahead, but at this gate take the second, less obvious gate to the right and at the end of the hedge turn left and on to the next field. Go through the gate and then follow the hedge up to the right to reach the Pateley Bridge road.

7. Cross the road and slightly off-set is a finger-post on the opposite side. Follow the wall now through four fields, to a stile into a private road. On the other side of this is another stile into an adjacent field through which the path runs parallel to the private lane. At the end of this is a stile which takes you into the other end of the lane. Turn left and then right, over a newly-built stone stile and pass a modern barn. At the far end of this, go through another gate into a small triangular field and head for the right-hand corner ahead, where the stile takes you into a narrow fenced path. Follow this down the hill to the road, and cross this through a stile and on to a footbridge over Thornton Beck. At the other side of the bridge continue straight ahead to a stile ahead, and after this turn left to re-join the path into Shaw Mills.

The
Long
Walks

Long Walk 1

Little Ribston – Plumpton

Distance: **9.5 miles**   *Map:* **OS Explorer 289**

Description: Easy walking, though muddy in places, especially in winter.

Pub: The Castle Inn, Spofforth (slightly off route).

Starting Point: **SE 386532.**

In the middle of Little Ribston, at the junction of the unclassified road to Spofforth with the B6164 Knaresborough to Wetherby road.

Boundary Notes: The Boundary in this area follows the River Nidd downstream to the Crimple, and then upstream along the Crimple.

1. Follow the road towards Spofforth for a third of a mile, and where the road bends left take the sign-posted track along a field side to the right. After two fields, the track becomes a path and continues beside a large hedge until it passes the water treatment works on the left. At the top of the treatment works the path turns first to the left, and then in a few yards right, leaving the works behind. Continue along the edge of the field through three fields and down York Hill to the Harrogate-Wetherby road (A661). Follow this to the left towards Wetherby for 250 yards, keeping on the grass verge as the road is busy and the traffic is fast, and then enter the farm yard of Crosper Farm.

Opposite: Boundary Stone 2

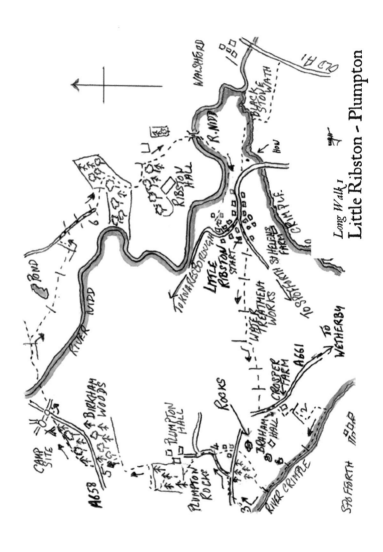

2. Walk straight ahead past several farm buildings and at the end, where a huge new barn has recently been built, turn left and make for a heavy gate to the right. Go through this, being sure to close the gate behind you. (**NB**. Animals getting onto the A661 would be very dangerous; farm yards are also dangerous for children.) Go directly down the field to a gate at the bottom where there is a stile on the left. Cross this stile and follow the hedge past three trees to another stile. Go over this, cross a dyke and then go directly across the field to the banks of the River Crimple.

There are several huge gritstone rocks about this area that are the sediment of a great river, which flowed from north to south millions of years ago, when the earth's tectonic plates were in very different positions. They are of the same type as those at Plumpton Rocks and some have names: one is called Hell Hole Stone, and another Holy Stone.

Spofforth Castle is half a mile downstream from the point where this walk joins the river. It was the home of the Percy family of Northumberland, and it was from this fortified manor house that Earl Percy led his army of Foresters to the fateful Battle of Towton during the Wars of the Roses. The Forest of Knaresborough was Lancastrian and it was a Yorkist victory. It was estimated that 50,000 men died on that winter day and no doubt many would have been Foresters.

(To visit the Castle Inn at Spofforth, turn left and follow the Crimple to the A661 and the village, and then retrace your footsteps.)

3. Turn right and follow the Crimple upstream for a mile and a half (this is the Forest Boundary), until it reaches the Follifoot road. Do not join the road here, but bear right up the side of Brown Hill Wood to the A661.

4. Cross the road as soon as possible and follow it east for 200 yards to a bridle road that leads left into the Plumpton Estate.

Plumpton was originally the seat of the de Plumptons and was a manor dating back to the Doomsday Book of 1086. It was purchased by Daniel Lascelles in the middle of the 18th century. Plumpton Hall itself was demolished many years ago, having been badly damaged by the Parliamentary Army soon after the Battle of Marston Moor. The imposing buildings that remain were once the stables, and have now been converted into private homes. The Plumpton Hunters, who currently own the estate, are a branch of the original family and represent the 28th generation. The amazing rocky grounds are thought to be the place from which the huge monolithic stones, which form the 'Devil's Arrows' near Boroughbridge, were quarried in the prehistoric past. The grounds were set out by Daniel Lascelles as a 'romantic garden' in about 1750. These still remain, and are open throughout the summer months at weekends.

5. Passing the estate gatehouse, continue along the drive for half a mile. Keep left where the estate road forks and then immediately enter a field on the left by a small gate for walkers. Continue across the field to another small gate and follow the path through the wood. The path opens out onto a wide track at a T-junction. Turn left here, and almost immediately right, past a pig run (this of course may not always be here). The path turns right after 200 yards towards a wood. At the wood turn left (well way-marked),

and continue to the end of the wood, where you turn right; keeping the wood on your right, reach a broad track at a T-junction, marked on the OS map as the Great Harbour. Take the broad track to the left, follow the field round to reach the corner of Birkham Wood. You follow with the wood to your right to reach the Harrogate and Knaresborough by-pass (A658).

6. Cross the road, keeping dogs and children under close control and continue, keeping Birkham Wood still on your right hand. The path leaves the wood to pass through the edge of the Lido campsite and on to the by-pass at the Grimbald roundabout. Go straight across the road and into a path which avoids walking along the busy road. Where the path rejoins the road from the Grimbald roundabout to Little Ribston, cross straight over and drop down the lane opposite to the bridge by the old Goldsborough Mill. (The route here is above the course of the Nidd which forms the Forest Boundary.) Follow the track towards Goldsborough and in a third of a mile turn off right, soon after passing under the electricity pylons, on a foot path that goes past a large pond after half a mile. Go over a stile and continue straight ahead to another stile and then along a ridge above the Nidd to a further stile. Cross this and turn left, keeping a hedge on your left, to join up with a very narrow tarmac road coming from Goldsborough. Turn right and follow this lane for a half a mile.

Goldsborough Hall was the home of the Hutton family, who were Knaresborough MPs in the days when it was a 'Rotten Borough' and had two Members of Parliament. It was later owned by the Lascelles family, until they finally settled at Harewood. The house then became a boys' Preparatory School and then a residential home, and is now a hotel.

Rudding Park

7. When this lane terminates, the footpath continues towards Ribston Park. The path enters a wood and then there is a clear well-marked route through the Park of Ribston Hall. The path has been diverted to avoid intrusion, and then joins the estate road to cross over the Nidd by a rather imposing bridge.

Ribston Hall was once the home of the Goodricke family who had bought it from the Duke of Suffolk soon after the dissolution of the Knights Templar. The estate and house passed into the ownership of Mr James Dent in the mid-nineteenth century and is now the private residence of Mr Charles Dent. There still remains a chapel of the Knights Templar, and in the grounds there is the remains of what is thought to be a jousting field. Also in the grounds there is an apple tree known as the Ribston Pippin, the tree from which all pippin apples are descended. The Ribston Pippin is part of the Harrogate Coat of Arms, with wheat sheaves on either side representing a wide rural district.

8. After crossing the Nidd, follow the drive of Ribston Hall towards Little Ribston and, where the drive and the river are close together, bear right and head for a field gate ahead. Pass through this and follow the line of trees over open land towards a cottage. The path enters the garden of the cottage and then leads out onto a narrow local lane. Turn left and, passing another cottage, join the main road (B6164). Turn left towards Wetherby, and in a quarter of a mile you will be at the end of the walk and at the point at which you started.

If you have any energy left, it is worth taking the path from Ribston east through South Park to Blackstone Wath. This is very close to the point at which the Forest Boundary Perambulation was historically begun, and is now a forgotten road which went from here to Ingmanthorpe. As you return, note the old tumuli in South Park, probably a Saxon burial place dating from before the Norman Conquest. There were at one time several of these tumuli, all with names: Peesbury Hill, Maunbury Hill, and How Hill.

There is a short stretch of the Crimple, between Blackstone Wath and the main road, (A168) called Mill Green where the ancient North Deighton corn mill was. The place now is private land but is identifiable by some tree planting.

Follifoot - Kirkby Overblow - Crimple

Distance: **9 miles**   *Map:* **OS Explorer 289**

Description: Mainly good going. The later stages of this Walk follow Short Walk 3.

Pubs: The Ratcliffe Arms and the Harewood Arms, Follifoot; the Shoulder of Mutton and the Star and Garter, Kirkby Overblow; the Travellers Rest, Crimple.

Starting Point: **SE 343525.**

The centre of Follifoot village, opposite the Harewood Arms. There is a bus service from Harrogate to Wetherby which goes through Follifoot.

The Walk could also begin at Kirkby Overblow (**SE 493324**).

Boundary Notes: The Boundary in this area follows the River Nidd downstream to the Crimple, and then upstream along the Crimple.

Before starting the walk, it is worth taking a look at the remarkable village cross at the top of the main street near to the old stocks in Follifoot. There is a distinct section at its the base that is exceptionally old. This section was discovered in the grounds of Rudding Park while work was being undertaken on the very beautiful chapel near the house and is thought to be of Celtic origin. After it was discovered, Capt. Everard Ratcliffe had the cross erected on its present site, and had it dedicated to the memory of his father Sir Joseph Ratcliffe. The crucifix at the top is also thought to be very old, although it is not known exactly when and where it was found.

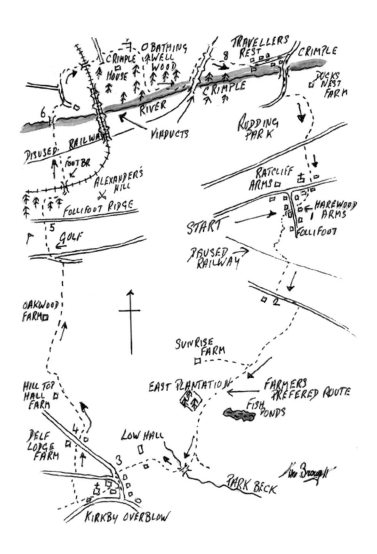

Long Walk 2
Follifoot - Kirby Overblow - Crimple

1. On the opposite side of the road to the pub there is a footpath which twists its way between cottages to a back lane. Go straight ahead and after 50 yards turn left on a broad grassy lane that runs parallel to the main village street. At the bottom of this there is a gate to the right, and the path leads on past Horse Pond Beck and wood (recently felled). At the end of the wood the path goes left, then right and left again, then straight on to join the old track bed of the railway.

2. Do not turn right along the track, but take the path that goes on a downward slope to cross the old railway line and up the embankment on the other side to a stile. Still keep south with a wood on your left, and at the end of the wood keep on past a line of old trees to join Haggs Road by Haggs Road Farm.

3. Turn left here (east) and follow the road for about five hundred yards and then take the sign-posted farm track right (south) to Lodge Wood, bearing right along an obvious farm track which passes through four fields without gates. The public right of way bears to the right, off this track, along a line of trees to Sun Rise Farm. However the farmer, Mr M. Liddle, has told me that he would prefer walkers to continue straight ahead at this point. If you choose this option, which is easy to follow and very satisfactory, the route passes a series of fishing lakes, not marked on the OS map (newly made!), due east of East Plantation, down a hill past a wood on your right and into the valley bottom. Where the public track goes left to follow Park Beck downstream, the footpath bears off to the right, into a corner, near a keepers' walk, where there is a stile and a footbridge over the beck. After crossing this, turn right and then in a hundred yards go half-left towards a driveway between a lodge cottage on the left and Low Hall.

Go through the gate and follow the footpath, keeping Low Hall park wall to your right. At the top of the field there is a stone stile taking you onto the main street of Kirkby Overblow.

It is thought that the name Overblow may come from the fact that this was at one time where iron was smelted.

4. Turn left and go past the Shoulder of Mutton, and a little further on, the Star and Garter. Turn right now to go directly to the church gates. Walk through the graveyard to a delightful stile and cross it into a private garden. The house to the left here is called St Helen's and is named after an ancient well. Walk past the goose pen and bear slightly right into a narrow fenced path at the top of which is a stile. Climb this and, ignoring the stile to your left, go straight ahead along a narrow fenced path and cross Walton Head Lane. Go right here and almost immediately left to follow a path which crosses the Pannal to Kirkby Overblow road near to Delf Lodge Farm.

5. Go over the stile on the other side of the road, cross a narrow part of the field and then follow the indistinct path left, with the hedge on your right, past Hill Top Hall Farm. The route goes along a very narrow but pleasant path, past a slight twist, and then the track ahead is straight all the way past the derelict Oakwood Farm. Just before the Harrogate by-pass (A 658) turn left on the old road, and then cross the busy main road with care. Take the right-hand bridleway opposite, with Pannal Golf Club on your left, and then cross the Follifoot Ridge Road, and take the path straight ahead.

7. In a few yards the green lane enters woodland. Cross through the wood on a muddy path and exit at a footpath gate. Turn right along a well-

trodden path to a bridge over the railway line. Go straight ahead here and through a piece of rough ground, which was the route of a now disused railway that went directly to Starbeck. The path ahead takes you over the Crimple on a substantial wood bridge, which is a replacement for one that was washed away in the 2007 floods. Continue up the farm track to a hedge and turn right to join the lower end of Fulwith Mill Lane.

8. Go up the hill and at the top where Fulwith Mill Lane bears left, go right (straight ahead). Bear right at the top of this towards a bridge over the railway, At the gates of St. Michael's Hospice, turn left, then after two cottages go right on an unmade footpath. Do not go left at the obvious gate, continue straight ahead, then turn right through Bathing Well Wood.

9. Where the path reaches the River Crimple at the bottom of the hill bear left and exit the wood. Keep along the side of the river and head for the path that goes under the far end of the now disused Old Crimple Viaduct. The path, which is sign posted, climbs steeply to go under the last arch and on into Crimple Wood.

10. The path through Crimple Wood leads to a stile and into a field with an obvious footpath, and then goes to a stile and enters Crimple Lane. Walk along the lane through the hamlet of Crimple, past the Travellers Rest pub, with views right to Rudding Park.

11. At the end of Crimple Lane, turn right onto the unclassified road over Collin Bridge towards Rudding. Follow the road up the hill and where it turns right at Rudding Park wall, turn left and follow the park wall to the

slope, to the left of a pair of big blue gates, that leads up to the Harrogate bypass (A658). Go across this busy road and over the stile ahead, and then straight ahead to the Follifoot road near the church. A short path opposite leads into the car park of the Harewood Arms, and the end of the walk.

Boundary Stone 4

North Rigton - Kirby Overblow - Weeton

Distance: **11 miles**	*Map:* **OS Explorer 297**

Description: ***Slightly hilly, but otherwise easy going.***

Pubs: The Square and Compass, North Rigton; the Shoulder of
Mutton and the Star and Garter, Kirkby Overblow.

Starting Point: **SE 280493**

The mini-roundabout by the Square and Compass in North
Rigton. There is a bus service from Harrogate to both North
Rigton and Kirkby Overblow.

Boundary Notes: The Walk passes close to Stone 5 (permission
to view required), is near to the Boundary along the
Swindon/Baffle Beck, and then follows it along the Wharfe,
past the site of Stone 6. Stone 4 can be viewed with a detour.

1. At the mini-roundabout, walk north-west up Rigton Hill for 100 yards.
On the right of the road a footpath passes through an ornamental gate, after
which a way-marked stile can be seen to your right. Go over the stile, and
continue straight ahead, ignoring another way-marked stile to your right, to
cross a small paddock to another stile. Cross five fields to a stile where the
path joins a lane coming in from the left. A public footpath signs the way
to Burn Bridge. Continue along this lane to the right until the lane enters a
field near to a small tarn, then pass through six fields, each with metal gates
to reach a point where the path turns sharp right towards Horn Bank Farm.

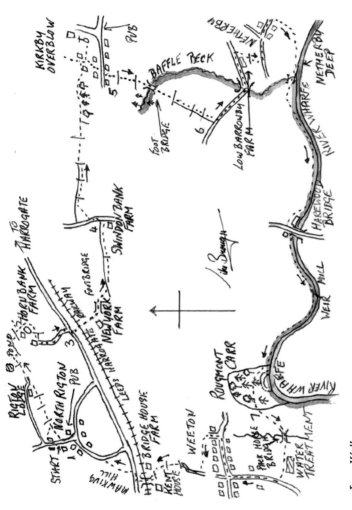

Long Walk 3
North Rigton – Kirby Overblow – Weeton

According to Harry Speight in his History of Kirkby Overblow, the old Roman Road from Catterick to Adel passed over the ridge here, coming south from Castle Hill near Pannel Ash. It is likely that there was a defensive lookout here, as the prospect in all directions is good. He also mentions that at the end of the 19th century there were still the remains of an ancient bathing place near here.

2. Turn diagonally left, down the eastern side of the farm, past a large cow barn and keeping a huge cylindrical slurry tank on your right, enter the concreted farmyard through a gate and walk towards the farm house. The way turns left past the side-door of the farm and goes down the obvious drive to the main road (A658).

3. Cross over the road here and turn right (towards Pool) and then almost immediately left onto a short track that leads to a pedestrian level-crossing over the railway. Checking carefully that the line is clear, cross the railway, and continue across a field to a stile passing New York Farm. Cross a substantially-built stone bridge over a tiny beck and bear right to a field gate 200 yards ahead. Go through the gate and follow the hedge on your left, until after another field you reach Swindon Bank Farm.

4. Cross the main Harrogate to Leeds road (A61) taking extra care, as it is a busy road. Walk 200 yards on the grass verge north towards Harrogate, to a stile on the right leading to a footpath across a field which often has horses in it. The path from here to Kirkby Overblow follows the contour of the north escarpment of the Wharfe Valley, commanding a continuous panoramic view towards Harewood. About half way along this path you pass a wooded hollow called Warholes at the top of which is Stone 5. To

view this, you must cross private farm land, and permission can be gained by contacting the farmer, Mr C Dowthwaite, High Snape Farm, Kirkby Overblow, Harrogate. Continue along your contour and at the third field pass a derelict water tank to a way-marked gate. Cross the stream, a small tributary of Swindon Beck, which is the actual Forest Boundary from here to the River Wharfe. As there is no right of way along Swindon Beck, continue to a stile at the edge of Kirkby Overblow, then turn right at another stile which leads into a private garden. This is a right of way, but as you head towards the house drive, watch out for the sign-posted footpath on the left which leads down to the road.

Stone 4 can be easily viewed from Walton Head Lane, which runs parallel with the contour path a little to the north.

5. Turn right at the road, and almost opposite to where the drive comes out there is a way-marked footpath to the left between high hedges. This leads down to a field, where it is best to choose the right-hand side of the hedge as it is less muddy. Keep to this hedge for half a mile, until it turns sharply left and at this point turn right towards a marker post close to a small wood. Here you cross a bridge over Swindon Beck, now called Baffle Beck, and then go straight ahead across the middle of four long fields to Swindon Grange Farm on the Netherby Road. The path is just discernable, and it leads to an iron gate, which is marked by a white painted arrow.

6. On reaching the road, turn left and walk for about three quarters of a mile to Low Barrowby Farm, and then follow the path south at the next gate for 200 yards away from the road to an iron gate and on for another 200 yards to a narrow lane. Turn left along the lane and where it joins a

Netherby Deep, Site of Boundary Stone 6

narrow metalled road, carry on straight ahead, past a camp site, to a gate on the right into a grassy path past a lovely old cottage, and along an obvious path to join the banks of the river Wharfe. Follow the river upstream to pass the point at which Baffle Beck (Swindon Beck) joins the river Wharfe. This is called Netherby Deep and is where Boundary Stone 6 once stood. The river is beguilingly lovely here, with a sandy beach, but don't be fooled - it is treacherous! I believe that Stone 6 may well be here at the bottom of the river under 35 feet of water. Continue upstream along the Wharfe, which is now the Forest Boundary, along a well-trodden footpath to reach the Harrogate to Leeds road (A61) at Harewood Bridge. Cross the road and follow the footpath upstream. It enters a house garden, but the way through is quite clear. Once through the garden, the route is along the river bank and in approximately a mile enters a wood called Rougemont.

Rougemont was the fortified manor house of Brian de l'Isle, a former governor of the Castle of Knaresborough in the 11th century. It was probably a wooden structure, although substantial earthworks are clearly visible. The place was almost certainly abandoned when the now-ruined Castle on Harewood Bank was built.

The Castle on Harewood Bank was owned by several medieval feudal families including the de Mescines, the de Romellies, and the Gascoignes. It is now part of the Earl of Harewood's estate.

7. After leaving Rougemont wood by the obvious path going to the west, cross a small field diagonally to a splendid packhorse bridge over Weeton Beck, and go past the Yorkshire Water treatment works to a lane. Follow the lane to the right and in just over half a mile enter the village of Weeton, at what was formerly the chapel. Turn right at the telephone kiosk, passing Juniper Farm on your left, and carry on past several houses and cottages, to turn left into Brook Lane at the end of white-painted fencing. Go to the end of the lane, through a pedestrian gap to the right of a field gate, and bear left into a private garden, where the owners have developed an extremely well-run vegetable plot. Climb the stile at the end, cross a small field and, after another stile, turn right into a delightful green lane, which winds up through several small fields past huge old willow trees. There is a slight zig-zag which takes you past Kent House Farm and onto the main road (A658). Cross this and, 25 yards to the right, go through a kissing gate to cross a field over Mawking Hill to reach the road into the village of North Rigton. Turn left and return to the Square and Compass and your starting point.

Long Walk 4
Lindley - Little Alms Cliff - Stainburn

Distance: **10 miles**   *Map:* **OS Explorer 297**

Description: A complicated route offering some challenging and very varied walking, with some hills, but particularly beautiful.

Starting Point: **SE 225483** or **SE 236522**

By car, take the A59 from Harrogate towards Skipton, and turn left onto the B6451 to Otley. Pass the hamlet of Bland Hill and climb to a crest of the hill close to the large radio mast on Norwood Edge. Drop down the hill past Lindley Reservoir turn left to park on the south side of Lindley Bridge. The walk can also begin at Little Alms Cliff, where there is a car park.

Boundary Notes: The Boundary in this area runs along the River Washburn, which is crossed by Lindley Bridge.

1. From the north side of Lindley Bridge take the path marked 'To Norwood Bottoms', by a cottage on the north side of the bridge, on a sharp bend in the road. The path leads through woodland to the reservoir dam. Half a mile beyond the dam, there is the attractive and noticeable valley, where the Greystones Beck flows into the reservoir under a substantial stone bridge. Cross the bridge and after 70 yards turn right off the main footpath to follow a fairly steep, winding path, which leads up to a stile and into a field. After going over the stile keep the dry stone wall on your right, until

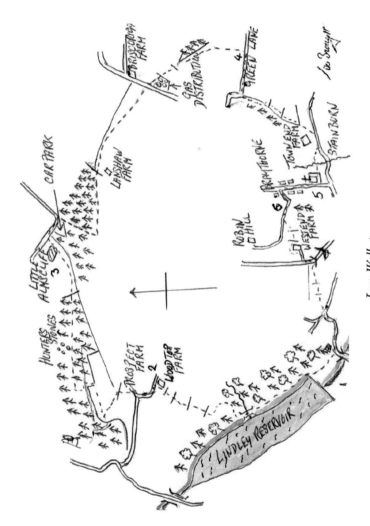

in a short distance the path turns right at a field boundary and goes north through 5 more metal gates and along the drive way of Wood Top Farm.

2. Turn left on the road here and in a very short distance the road goes right and then left. At this second bend, walk north up the drive of Prospect House Farm. There are two distinctive trees in this field, and at the second go through a gate and then turn left (west) towards Norwood Edge plantation. Ahead there is another gate by a small stream, and here the path is indistinct, but go straight ahead towards a corner of the woodland, following the remains of a dry stone wall on your right. In the corner of the wood there is a gate with a path leading from the field you are in. Do not follow the path into the wood, but turn right through clumps of rushes to a stile into the wood ahead. As soon as you have crossed this stile, turn left and follow the wall up to a track. Turn left here and in 10 yards right up a steep embankment to reach the path that passes the Hunters Stones. Upon reaching this higher path, turn right and follow it as it runs fairly straight through woodland for the next mile and a half. It passes Hunters Stones, and is interesting because there are a number of Boundary Stones which are unlike any of the others referred to in this book.

These stones are short and stubby, and bear only the letter 'F', and are actually marked 'BS' on the OS map. They are a slightly sad monument to the losers of the past, and mark the 'Copy Holders' Boundary. They were placed there between 1770 and 1775 during the time when the Forest was being carved up following the Enclosure Act, after which it would cease to exist. It is not possible to stand in the way of progress, but many of the old Foresters lost grazing rights which the ancient laws of the forest had granted them. For them, life would become yet harder.

Alms Cliff Crag

3. The path leads past the evocative Little Alms Cliff, with its pre-historic 'cup and ring' markings, and joins Broad Dubb Road. Follow the road to the right towards Beckwithshaw, as far as the corner, and at the car park (which is the alternative start) turn right to enter the track that goes through the wood. In a quarter of a mile, where this opens out onto farm land and the main track bears right, turn left, keeping the wood on your left, towards Lanshaw Farm. Here you take the metalled farm drive to the B6161 road from Beckwithshaw. Go straight across the road to follow the track which goes past a gas distribution station. This track passes through two metal gates and soon becomes a pleasant grassy footpath, passing a small wood on your left. From here, on a clear day, you can pick out the plumes of steam and the cooling towers of three power stations on the horizon, and much nearer the spectacular form of Alms Cliff Crag.

4. Towards the end of the wood the green field path bears slightly right to reach a gate onto Greenmires Lane. Turn right here, and then after four hundred yards, at a distinct right turn in the road, turn left onto a bridle path, which leads first through a narrow strip of woodland and then into a field and, still keeping the wood on your right, keep ahead ignoring a stile on the right. Go through a metal gate and along the side of a small sike until you reach a small metal footpath gate which leads into a little spinney. Pass through this to join Low Lane and turn right and walk down the road, past Town End Farm, towards the village of Stainburn. 200 yards beyond a house called Valley View, climb the stile on your right and make your way diagonally left to pass on the north side of a ruined barn. After passing the barn continue down the field towards Stainburn Beck, and at the bottom turn right to go through a squeeze-stile, and then immediately left to cross the beck. Continue ahead past a large tree, and through another field to a stile into the graveyard of Stainburn Church.

5. Go through the church yard, leave by the main gate, and turn right along Church Lane to Braythorn. As you walk up the main street of the hamlet, you will see before you an old small disused chapel (1836) now converted into a cottage, at the junction of a narrow un-surfaced lane. Turn left to follow this lane towards Robins Hill, and after about a third of mile there is on your left a well-marked footpath with a stile, soon after beginning a fairly steep climb. Climb the stile and cross the field towards a post indicating where your next stile is. Climb this and go straight ahead to reach the edge of West End Farm.

6. The path has been diverted here, but the new route has been well marked and passes through a small plantation before rejoining the driveway. Turn right on the drive to reach the B6161. Turn left at this, crossing first

to face oncoming traffic, and after 50 yards take a footpath to the right at a sharp left-hand bend. Keep more or less to the contour, passing a number of large gorse bushes, and then make your way down the field towards a point where the fencing ahead comes to an inexplicable end in the middle of the field! Head west from here to the next field boundary, which is a ditch with a clapper bridge over it and a stile, indicated by a post with a yellow-marked top. Then go straight ahead, across a narrow field which usually has sown crops. After this the path crosses another field diagonally, down to where there is a wall-stile at the side of a metal field gate. After crossing this, bear slightly to the right past a ruined barn and up to the corner of the field, to a footpath sign at Pill White Lane. Turn left and follow the quiet road down the hill to a T-junction, and then turn right until after 450 yards you reach Lindley Bridge, and the welcome sight of your car.

Long Walk 5
Fewston - Swinsty - Timble

Distance: **10 miles**   Map: **OS Explorer 297**

Description: A fairly hilly walk, moderately strenuous, and muddy in places.

Pub: The Timble Inn at Timble (book in advance if food is required); Hopper Lane Inn, Fewston, a little off route.

Starting Point: **SE 169553**

The car park at Blubberhouses at the western end of Fewston Reservoir by the A59. There is a bus service from Harrogate to Skipton along the A59.

Boundary Notes: In this area the Boundary follows the River Timble. The Walk passes Stone 8.

The car park is the site of a long-lost pub, the Frankland Arms, named after an old land-owning family. It closed through lack of business when the flax industry went into decline.

1. Take the short path onto the A59 and turn right. Follow the verge over the bridge that crosses the river Washburn and then take the path away from the road to the side of the reservoir and follow this all the way along the north-eastern side of the water.

Fewston Reservoir is part of the Leeds Water Works' Washburn supply, and was completed in 1891. It was the first of the Washburn Valley reservoirs and was followed by Swinsty Reservoir and later Lindley

Fewston - Swinsty - Timble

Wood Reservoir. The last, Thruscross, was built in 1965 and covers the old deserted village of West End.

2. Just before the path reaches the Fewston dam, it turns north to go round the edge of the keeper's cottage land, and then down stone steps to cross the road that comes from Fewston village to Timble. After re-entering the Water Board land at the other side of the road, there is a choice. The path to the left is a zig-zag and is suitable for wheel chairs, while to the right the path is more direct. Continue along the north side of Swinsty Reservoir to the designated car park and picnic place.

On the other side of the water and hidden in the trees is Swinsty Hall, which is steeped in legend. It is a large house, with many chimneys and gables, tucked away in woodland. There is a tale of a poor local weaver called Robinson, who once lived at a place near Timble called Green Well, who went to London and made his fortune, and used his money to build the Hall. Colourful as this is, it is probably no more true than the tales of witches in Timble Gill and Fewston, who were charged by Fairfax, tried at York, and acquitted.

3. Cross a small spur of the reservoir here by taking the road (Smithson Lane) and after crossing the causeway, rejoin the waterside path to the dam at Swinsty Cottage. Cross the dam and at its far side take the permissive footpath to the south, and then go on to a stile at the side of the River Washburn. Ignore the substantial farm bridge over the Washburn, but climb the stile and follow the riverside downstream to a new wooden footbridge over the Timble Beck.

Until the 2007 flood there was a delightful miniature arched pack horse bridge here, called The Adamson Memorial Bridge, in memory of Arthur Adamson, a respected member of the Ramblers Association.

4. After climbing the stile by the river, cross the replacement Adamson Bridge, and take the path that climbs a short steep embankment and then bears right to head for a dry stone wall. On reaching this, turn right and make for an ancient and stunted oak tree with a yellow way marker. Turn left here and follow the bottom of an old wood.

5. At the end of the wood, turn right towards a stone wall with another yellow marker. Continue up the hill, with a tiny brook to your left, and then farm buildings to your left. Cross a small field to a stone stile and enter the farmyard of Washburn Farm. Turn right and at the other end of the farmyard enter a walled farm track, through a gate, and then in a field down the hill to the corner of a small wood. Cross a bridge over a tributary of Timble Beck, and where the track turns right into a field, continue ahead to a gate with a stile. Cross a small stream and continue on a clear path that follows the contour of Redding Hill to a field gate. The marked arrow shows that you go through the gate and turn right. Climb a short, fairly steep hill and, with a dry stone wall to your right, reach a stile which leads to the site of a bridge swept away in 2007. Negotiate the beck with care! After crossing, there is a way-marked path, which after three more fields joins an ancient walled green track leading to the hill-top village of Timble.

6. After passing the pub, at the western end of the village take the sign-posted path south, by a stile close to the village information board. The path soon becomes an ancient and almost forgotten green lane, and takes

you back to Timble Gill Beck, but a little further upstream. The whole of the beck is part of the actual boundary of the Forest. There was a bridge here too, until 2007! Cross the beck with caution; the crude steps are slippery and the place where the bridge was is steep. Once over the gill, turn right, ignoring a stile to your left, and make for the opposite right-hand corner of the field. The stile is in the corner and not visible until you are upon it. Squeeze through, and then, keeping the wall on your right, continue to the gate, then turn right and past a small barn. Go through the gate ahead keeping the field boundary close to your left, but ignoring the footpath that turns off through a field towards the gill. The second gate ahead leads into a very narrow field towards Shaw Hall.

7. As Shaw Hall becomes visible ahead, a notice directs you slightly right to a way-marked footpath gate. Do not take the obvious way-marked path that goes through a thin strip of trees, but only two or three yards to the right of this gate is an unmarked stile that is quite difficult to spot. Take this, and then follow a field boundary north towards a very well maintained barn. Continue past this and on into Prospect House farmyard. Where the farm drive from the road comes in from the left, turn right through a gate with a yellow way-marker and head for the right side of a spur of hedge close to the now tiny Timble Beck.

At this point you may decide that it is worthwhile going over to the corner of the field to your left, near where the Timble to Otley road makes a right-hand turn. There is a large bush on the roadside, and close by is Forest Boundary Stone 8, which is unusually inscribed 1825. The original would have been marked 1767 and must have been lost,

Boundary Stone 8

probably during road improvements, and replaced by someone who cared.

8. Now walk diagonally right, across the field from the last gate to a point where a dry stone wall ahead meets one coming south from Lane End Farm. At this corner go diagonally across the next field, through a gate and then follow a wall on your left to enter the road from Fewston, close to a ruined barn. Turn right here towards Timble, and in 25 yards follow the fork to the left. Continue along the road for one third of a mile to where the drive of Ridge Top Farm comes in on your right. This is the corner of Beechcroft Moor plantation on Timble Ridge.

9. Go over the stile on your left, and take the path into the wood. Adjacent to the stile is a gate, but do not take this as the path from it will take you through the wood to the wrong place. After 25 yards there is a post with yellow arrows, and you here take the middle one down through the wood. About half way through the wood, the path crosses a fairly substantial forest track. Continue straight across this, and through a part where the ground is very wet, especially in winter. At the northern end of the wood the path crosses a wooden foot bridge over Thackray Beck, and then goes immediately over a stone stile to continue along a walled and wet green track.

10. Go through the gate at the northern end of the track, and keep the fence on your right, passing a line of hawthorn bushes. After a short distance the path is indicated half-left towards a distinctive old oak tree and on to a stile. The path ahead is full of reeds, but the way forward is clear. Another gate, and the now-indistinct track of an old walled grassy road continues, with the field boundary on your right. The old Roman road from Aldborough to Ilkley crossed here, as a line of trees gives testament. After a difficult gate continue to a stile, and at an opening in the wall on the left, make for a small wicket gate. Go through this and down the hill near Hill Top House and back to the car park at Blubberhouses.

Long Walk 6
Blubberhouses Moor and the Roman Road

Distance: **7.5 miles**   *Map:* **OS Explorer 297**

Description: The first half is easy going. The second half is strenuous and challenging, over rough moorland and tufty grass.

Pub: The Timble Inn, Timble (check hours and book ahead if food is required) which could be visited at the start or end of the walk.

Starting Point: **SE 166530**

The small parking place next to the plantation on the rough road that runs west, past Sourby Farm, from the junction of the road from Timble with the road south from Blubberhouses.

Boundary Notes: The Walk passes Stones 9, 11 and 12.

1. Continue along the rough road for a short distance to take a fork to the left towards Ellarcarr Pike, sign-posted Denton, Middleton, Ilkley.

There are several old boundary stones along this stretch ,with the letters 'D' for Denton, 'F' for Frankland, 'M' for Middleton and 'T' for Thackray. Denton and Middleton are parish boundaries and Frankland and Thackray local land-owning families who make up the intriguing history of the Fewston and Timble District. There is also a stone marked with two '++'. This is likely to be a boundary to a 'Right of Pasture' granted to the de Plumptons by Henry VI for services rendered at the time of the uprising at Topcliffe, when Earl Percy was murdered for being too zealous in his tax collecting.

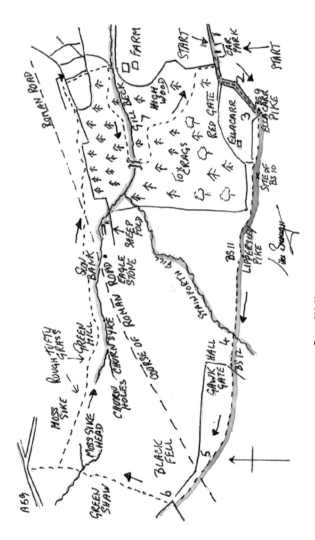

Long Walk 6
Blubberhouses Moor and the Roman Road

Boundary Stone 9

2. Ignore the ladder stile to the left and go through a metal gate over a cattle grid. In a hundred yards the track turns half right and passes three Boundary Stones, about twenty yards apart. In less than half a mile from the car park, at the end of a dry stone wall, at what is known as Ellarcarr

Pike you can see Stone 9. This has a bench mark and like Stone 8, is marked 1825. It seems likely that the original must have somehow been lost and that this is a replacement. There is a stone marked 'A' for Askwith behind Boundary Stone 9.

3. At Stone 9 the route bears slightly right to the west. Ignore the drive to Ivy House and follow the wall side onto open moor. Continue on westwards, to pass Stone 11 on Lippersley Edge.

I have not found Stone 10, but I am reasonably certain that, given a warm sunny day and plenty of time, it may well be found. It was photographed lying down a number of years ago by a visitor to the area.

4. Continuing in the same direction across the head of Stainforth Gill you will reach Gawk Hall Gate, where the earthbound stone at the foot of the gate post on your left is Stone 12. It is unlike any of the other Boundary Stones, as it is insignificant, almost concealed, but marked with its K F and 1767.

5. Quite near to here the path crosses a footpath which comes up from the old Roman road from the north-east and which leads south-west to Ilkley, passing an old way-marker stone inscribed '14 M RIPPON' and 'ILKLEY 3 M'.

6. The route and the Forest Boundary continue to Little Gate and Green Shaw Head. Go through the gate here and turn right to head north between Black Fell and Green Shaw down the moorland bridle path. Thirty yards past Mossy Sikes Dike take the footpath, marked on the OS

map but scarcely recognisable on the ground, which turns sharp right, and climb the hill to the south-south-east, keeping the grouse butts away to your left. The path crosses the shoulder of the moor, over Greenhill, and then drops down to Churn Holes Dike. It passes Sun Bank and goes down the hill to join up with the old Roman road. Follow this for 25 yards, and then bear right onto an access path that turns slowly away from the Roman road right towards Gill Beck (SE161541). The path enters a field on the side of the moor and then a wood. Go through the wood to where a distinct track crosses and turn right. The track turns gradually to the left, to a bridge over Thackray Beck. Go over the bridge and after 50 yards turn left onto a permissive track through the wood.

Gill Beck becomes Thackray Beck and is one of the main supply streams of Fewston Reservoir. The Thackray Farm, from which the beck takes its name, is now deep beneath the waters of the reservoir. Thackray, or Thackeray, is a name that occurs frequently in the Forest, and is linked with the writer William Makepeace Thackeray, author of Vanity Fair, who is commemorated in Hampsthwaite Church.

7. The track through the wood opens out into a clearing, where Sourby Farm can just be seen ahead. Turn right here and follow a well marked Water Board permissive right-of-way up the hill. This track twists and turns through lovely woodland, eventually reaching the lane where cars can be parked close to the drive end of Sourby Farm, and the place where the walk started.

Long Walk 7
Blubberhouses - Rocking Hall

Distance: **11 miles**   *Map:* **OS Explorer 297**

Description: Mixed challenges, some rough moor, some wet and peaty, some easy going.

Pub: Hopper Lane Inn, Fewston, not on the route but close to the start and finish.

Starting Point: **SE 169553**

The car park at Blubberhouses at the western end of Fewston Reservoir by the A59. There is a bus service from Harrogate to Skipton along the A59.

Boundary Notes: In this area the Boundary follows the Black Sike up to Cort How. Stone 15 is at Rocking Hall.

The car park is the site of a long lost pub, the Frankland Arms, named after an old land-owning family. It closed through lack of business when the flax industry went into decline

1. Leave the car park and follow the A59 road left to the junction with the unclassified B road to Otley. Cross over to follow the minor road, Hall Lane, past Blubberhouses Hall. At the first sharp right hand turn in this road, take the unmade cart track straight ahead up Lime Kiln Hill and follow this west for about a mile, to where it joins up with Kex Gill Road. After a very short distance, turn off this onto a marked footpath on the left. This path goes through Kex Gill below the gritstone crags and emerges from the steep-sided gill onto the A59. Go west along this for a short

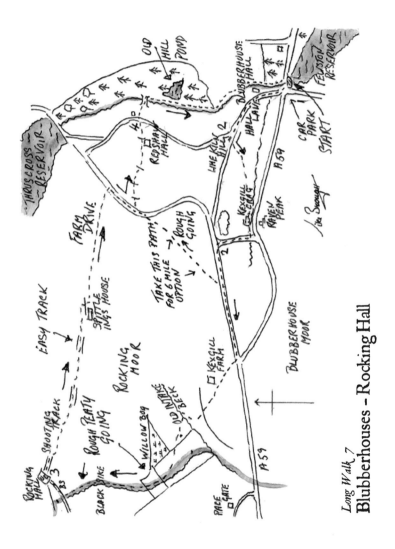

Long Walk 7
Blubberhouses – Rocking Hall

Boundary Stone 15

distance, and then turn right (north) on the minor road that leads from the A59 at the top of the gill, passing the entrance of a hidden quarry where very high quality silica sand was extracted for glass-making until it closed a few years ago.

2. Where the road bears right (east) towards Thruscross, turn sharp left along the now disused road towards Kex Gill Farm. Re-join the A59 and almost immediately turn off onto the drive way of Kex Gill Farm. At the farm take the footpath that goes west on the north side of Kirk Hill and then by Old Intake Beck to turn north west along the boundary of the National Park, which leads to Black Sike, keeping Willow Bog well to your right. Follow Black Sike for just under two miles, through Shepherds

Close, until it crosses the Duke of Devonshire's shooting road. The going is very rough, with peat hags. Turn right on this to reach Rocking Hall.

Rocking Hall consists of two stone-built shooting lodges with two huge rocks, one on top of the other, in between. It is said that the top one was at one time a Druid rocking stone although it has not rocked for over 150 years. The shooting lodges were originally built by the Nicholsons of Roundhay Hall in Leeds, soon after the Knaresborough Forest was enclosed in 1770 and the family became owners of a large tract of moor. The lodges are interesting for two reasons. One has a carved stone face above its door, and the other has Boundary Stone 15 as its front door step. Stone 15 should have been at Cort How, about a half of a mile west, but was clearly 'utilised' during the building of the lodge in 1775. The whole of Rocking Hall is surrounded by a dry stone wall with gates. The whole of Rocking Hall Moor is now part of the Bolton Abbey estate of the Duke of Devonshire.

3. From Rocking Hall, follow the shooting track east-south-east to Spittle Ings House. After climbing the high stile, the farm drive to the left continues to join Kex Gill Road just north of Burnt House. Turn right along this and after passing the entrance to Burnt house take the signposted footpath off to the left which runs parallel and to the north of Redshaw Gill, following a tumble-down dry stone wall on the left, and passing through four fields before following the same wall on the other side along one more field. Pass a gate stile and follow diagonally left to enter an old green road to Redshaw Hall. At Redshaw Hall go through a waymarked gate and over a stone stile, and then continue along the old green path to join Bank Dyke Lane.

4. Turn left, and then in 15 yards right at a footpath sign, descend a stile with stone steps, and continue down a steeply sloping field to enter the wood. The path drops down to the beck and a foot bridge. Ignore the path to the left here (which would take you up the opposite side of the valley), but instead turn right, keeping to the side of the River Washburn. In a quarter of a mile the main footpath, which is part of the Dales Way, bears left to climb out of the valley, but do not take that, instead keep to the impressive permissive path, with its huge beech trees which follow the Washburn like a great avenue.

Note the extraordinary way that the enormous trunks of these giants are shaped. They must have formed a hedge some two hundred years ago and even today it is possible to see that that hedge has been 'laid' in the old traditional method.

5. Pass Blubberhouses cricket field, and go up steps to the main road and the car park.

The cricket field and its pavilion are on the site of the huge, infamous, and demolished, Westfield Flax Mill where children, orphans and waifs were subjected to long hard hours and cruel conditions. There are a few remains at the far side of the ground.

Long Walk 8
Keld Houses - Green How Hill

Distance: **8 miles**   *Map:* **OS Explorer 298**

Description: Mainly easy walking, although fairly difficult in parts. Care needed in the region of the old lead mines, especially with children and dogs.

Starting Point: **SE 105638**

The hamlet of Keld Houses near the village of Greenhow on the B6265 Pateley Bridge to Grassington road.

Boundary Notes: The Walk follows the Boundary from near Keld Houses to Lord's Seat. Stone 18 is at Lord's Seat.

---

1.   Follow the B6265 road west and, after passing the last house on the right-hand side of the road, go through a gate to the left and follow the green track across Craven Moor towards Sun Side Allotment.

The whole of this area is pock-marked like a lunar landscape with ancient 'bell pit' heads. These are the scars of many periods of early lead mining; some of the bell pits date back to Roman times. Beware! Some of the more recent ones are still open, and although most have a covering of rotten timber or corrugated iron, they are many fathoms deep and dangerous. Keep children and pets under supervision. Some of the grooves and hollows, and some of the old buildings, are interesting and remain as a monument to the hard lives of those whose life created these industrial relics. Mining came to an end in this district in the early years of the 20th century, due mainly to a drop in the

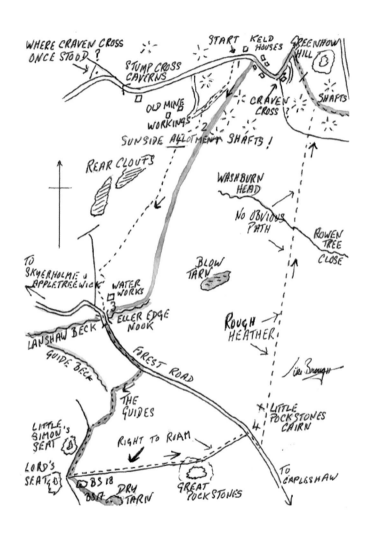

*market value of lead, and the fact that any demand for it could be met
from other parts.*

*This area was the scene of a bitter dispute between two local
landowners, Sir Thomas Willington White of Eagle Hall, and John
Yorke of Gouthwaite Hall, whose interest lay primarily in the mineral
wealth beneath the ground. Due to the dispute, which ultimately had
to be settled in court, the Boundary here has been altered, and Stones 21
to 25 were 'cast down'. The whole of this part of the walk, from the
mine workings to Lord's Seat, is the old Boundary of the Forest.*

2. The path swings first slightly to the right near to some derelict mine
buildings, and then left before crossing a dry stone wall by a stile. Pass over
this and continue in a more or less straight line, with the western side of a
hill called Rear Clouts to the right. As the path drops down the gentle
slope towards a wall ahead, it turns left and continues to a Water Works
building. Go past this, and through a metal gate into a green track called
Forest Road at a place called Eller Edge Nook.

*Originally the Boundary is said to have gone from Lord's Seat over
Rear Clouts to Mungo Gill and then to the place where the Craven
Cross once stood. No one really knows exactly where the Craven Cross
actually stood, but I believe that it was on a small triangle of land at a
bend in the B6265 a little west of Stump Cross Caverns. Examination
of this triangle of ground reveals a distinct hump in the centre, which
could be due to the base stones. The fact that the nearby show cave is
called 'Stump Cross' could be significant.*

Boundary Stone 18

3. Continue to the left over a bridge crossing Lanshaw Beck, and follow the wall on the right in the direction of Little Pock Stones for a third of a mile to a stile in the wall. Go over the stile and cross a difficult-to-follow stretch

of very rough but way-posted moor, called the Guides. It is always possible to spot the next white way-post, although upon reaching each it is necessary to be observant. When finally you reach the wall on the other side, turn left and follow this up first to Little Simon's Seat, and then Lord's Seat.

If you climb the wall corner at Lord's Seat, you can see a huge boulder, on the south side of which is inscribed '18', 'KF', '1767'. This is unlike the usual Boundary Stones, as it is not purpose-made.

4. Follow the wall now to the left to Little Pock Stones, passing Great Pock Stones *en route*. From Little Pock Stones, go over the wall and follow it round to pick up the long straight path that heads almost due north directly towards the Green How Mast and Green How Hill. Go over the wall here, and at the footpath turn left, through a lead mine area known as Galloway Pasture and on to the B6265, following the road towards Grassington to reach the starting point at Keld Houses.

Padside - Capelshaw Beck - Thruscross Reservoir

Distance: **12 miles**   *Map:* **OS Explorer 298**

Description: *Mostly easy walking with a rough section. As far as section 8 the route follows that of Short Walk 10. An OS map and a compass are important.*

Pub: The Stonehouse Inn (only slightly off route).

Starting Point: **SE 147602**

About half way along the minor road from Blubberhouses to Greenhow, Braithwaite Lane turns off to the east, and passes the drive of Padside Hall. You can park close to the drive, but avoid blocking the field gate.

Boundary Notes: Fall Beck is the Boundary of the Forest, and soon becomes Padside Beck and then Darley Beck before flowing into the Nidd. Stone 29 is at the start of the Walk, and it passes Stone 27, and Stone 26.

---

1. Walk north along Braithwaite Lane towards a bridge which crosses Fall Beck, and just before the bridge there is a wall stile on the right. From this, Stone 29 can clearly be seen standing among gorse bushes a few yards west of the beck and about 50 yards away. The path that crossed this field has now been diverted.

2. After viewing Stone 29, return to where you have parked and go along the drive of Padside Hall. A way-marked diverted path turns off the drive

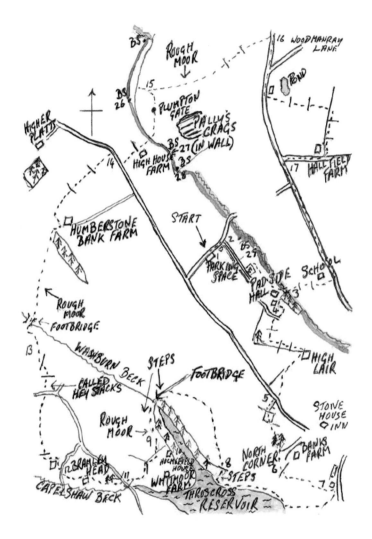

Long Walk 9
Padside - Capelshaw Beck - Thruscross Reservoir

left, where a line of huge spruce trees ends at stone gate pillars and an area of wood begins. It goes down the side of the wood keeping close to the dry-stone wall. Climb the wood stile to enter a field at the bottom of the wood. Continue another 20 yards, still with the wall, and turn right past an old tree to pass on the right side of two ponds. The path passes just below the Hall to a reach a stile ahead at the bottom of another wood close to the beck side.

3. Climb the wooden stile and turn to the right, with the fence at the edge of the wood on your right, up the steep hill and, after a dilapidated stile, pass close by the perimeter wall of the Hall.

4. A few yards past Padside Hall there is a cottage. Turn left onto its drive, and follow this for a short distance up to a sharp bend. Follow the bend right, and climb a stone stile (unmarked) on your left. Walk straight ahead and go between a pair of gate posts and up to a metal gate by a small clump of trees. At the gate, turn left to cross two fields. Don't take the path ahead (which continues to High Lair), but instead turn right at a stone stile and, after two fields, reach the Greenhow Hill road.

5. Go straight across the road and into a field opposite. Walk straight ahead with the dry stone wall on your left. At the corner of this field, go diagonally left and at the next field diagonally again to a stile which enters a recently planted birch wood. The diagonal line continues through the middle of the wood and on in the same line to reach the tiny hamlet of Thruscross and North Corner Barn (now converted into a private house).

6. Go straight ahead, still on the same line, across a piece of common rough pasture, past a way-marker post to a ladder-stile. On the other side of this, go ahead keeping the wall on your left, and keep following it as it turns gradually left. There are way-markers which direct you to the left of an overgrown hedge, and on past a redundant squeeze-stile.

7. The path reaches the wall of a house with a gate marked private. Turn right here, past an old tree in the garden, and down the field past an electricity pole with a way-marker, to a gate onto the old road across the valley. Where this road disappears into the dark depths of the reservoir, turn right, and keep on with Thruscross Reservoir to your left.

8. Stay by the water until the path moves away from the reservoir at a wood. Go up the side of the wood, on a path with rough steps and over a ladder-stile out onto the open moor. The permissive path is clear with marker-posts, and where it is a bit muddy in winter there are stepping-stones. On the open moor there is a ladder-stile and a post with way-markers. (At this point the route diverges from Short Walk 10)

9. Do not be tempted to take a path to the left that descends back into the wood, but instead keep straight ahead past two small hills, Near and Far Comb Hills, and by a noticeable outcrop of rock on your right, drop down the fairly steep hill, with the wood on the left, to the bridge at the top end of the reservoir. Climb the steps on the other side of the bridge, over the ladder-stile and enjoy the wild scenery from the top.

> *The bench at the top of the steps was provided by Rene Houseman (née*
> *Verity) and her brother John, who farmed at Whitmoor Farm, in*
> *memory of Victor and Annie their father and mother who particularly*
> *loved the view from this place. It is said that they frequently walked*
> *here on summer evenings, and before sitting down to enjoy the view*
> *would always take a drink from the crystal water of nearby Lady Well.*

10.   Continue on the permissive path, which crosses Whit Moor with marker-posts to a stone stile by a gate. Go over this stile, turn right and, keeping the wall on your right, reach another stone stile in the corner. Go through this and turn left to join the Whitmoor Farm road, where you turn right to reach Whit Moor road at the top of Dukes Bank. Alternatively, there is also a popular path that remains in the reservoir wood, though it is steep and muddy in places at first.

> *If the wood path is chosen, it passes the very romantic ruin of*
> *Holmefield House, which was a shooting lodge built by the Reverend*
> *William Roundell soon after acquiring the land in 1778, after the*
> *Forest enclosure. The open moor to the north of the Washburn arm of*
> *Thruscross Reservoir is to this day called Roundell's Allotment. The*
> *land was bought for its game shooting.*

11.   If you have joined the road from the 'permissive' route, the farm drive joins the Whit Moor Road at the top of Duke's Hill. Take the sign-posted footpath to the right that runs parallel to, but above, Capelshaw Beck. If you have chosen the path through the wood close to the reservoir, you will join the road at the bottom of Duke's Hill. Climb the hill, and towards the top turn left onto the sign-posted footpath. The path passes a delightful small waterfall on the right. Past this, the path goes along the bottom of a

group of large old trees to a stile past a fine old dales house. Over another stile, turn right up through a paddock by the house and then turn left to a stone stile. The way is straight ahead and towards a line of stunted trees, that long ago was a hedge, at the side of a small stream. Keep the stream on your left as you head for the top right-hand corner of a large farm shed, and then turn left to a stile just past an electricity line. This leads to the drive of Lane Bottom Farm at Bramley Head, which is followed onto the road.

There is a small bridge over the beck to the left, and it is said that a local man called John Breakes left £5 in his will to have it built.

12. At the road, go right and then in 25 yards left into the drive of Brays Croft Farm. As soon as you leave the road, turn right with a barn on your left, and follow the farm track left to go round the barn. In 50 yards the track turns sharp right through a metal gate and goes up the hill past Garth Crook to Hey Stack near Red Gate. Where the stile comes out onto the lane, there is a sign-post pointing you across the lane, and to a gate slightly to the right. Go straight ahead here through the middle of the field to a gate and after this still ahead to another gate. Follow close by the wall and go over the stone stile on your left, though this is not easy to spot.

Always take extra care where you put your feet at nesting time in spring, as there are likely to be ground-nesting wild birds which are difficult to see. In this and several of the following sections there are likely to be sheep with lambs, so always keep dogs on a lead.

13. The way through the bracken is ill-defined, but keep straight ahead, due north, for 100 yards, then bear slightly left for a quarter of a mile until

Boundary Stone 27

joining the Washburn at a wooden footbridge. Go over the bridge and pick up another ill-defined path through the bracken, heading north-north-east across Hoodstorth Allotment. Half way across this difficult section there is a rocky area, but keep right of this, and as you approach the top you will be getting closer to a pine wood on your right. The path finally reaches Humberstone Farm, entering it by a gate on the right, still with the pine wood on your right. In 10 yards, and before the farm house, turn left through a gate into a small paddock. Ignoring the gate on the left, go to the far end and through a gate into a field. There is a large wood ahead, but turn half right towards a field gate (north). Go on to another field gate and, as you head for the gate out onto the Redlish Road, be sure to keep the small steam well to your left and head on a direct diagonal.

There are numerous families who have lived and worked this area of the upper Washburn for generations. They have run inns, worked blacksmith shops, run cotton and flax-mills and farmed the land, and even today their names occur. As can be seen by the elegance of the houses, their lives have sometimes been prosperous, but also sometimes a terrible struggle, but they are always proud of their lovely valley.

14. Upon reaching the gate onto the Redlish Road, turn right away from Greenhow, follow the road for about 250 yards and then turn left into the drive of High House Farm. Go straight past the farm house and through a gate into a field. Keeping the field wall on your right, make for another gate straight ahead which takes you onto the open moor.

As you pass through the field, if you glance over the wall on your right you will see Forest Boundary Stone 27, laid down and now part of the dry stone wall which separates the adjacent field from the open moor. The farmer at High House may grant permission to go and inspect the stone if requested. It is unusual for a Boundary Stone to be part of a dry-stone wall, but its inscription faces out into the field.

The path passes close by a standing stone, which is marked with a '+' and the letter 'R', and which is known as Plumpton Gate. It marks the edge of a 'Right of Pasture' granted to Sir Robert Plumpton by Henry VI for 'his great and agreeable services'. In April 1489 an insurrection at Topcliffe near Thirsk led to the murder of Earl Percy, Earl of Northumberland at 'Maiden Bower', near Cod Beck, and Sir Robert was required to subdue it. The trouble had begun because the people were being asked to pay too much in taxes to support the war in France. Lord Percy had been made the King's Tax Collector and was considered too vigilant. The Percy family had found themselves on the losing side in the Wars of the Roses, and were keen to ingratiate themselves with the King in the hope of regaining their confiscated lands. Sir William took a small army of Foresters and it took three years to bring the matter to a conclusion.

15.   Continue past the Plumpton Gate standing stone in a northerly direction towards Jordan Bog. Just before the bog turn right on a footpath that leads to Nanny Black Hill in an easterly direction. If visibility is good, aim towards a clump of trees on the skyline. The path is fairly easy to follow, with seven white marker-posts, eventually reaching the first of three fields leading to Foldshaw Lane. Keep the wall on the right.

Where the path reaches Jordan Bog, look over the wall to see Stone 26.

16. Upon reaching Foldshaw Lane, turn right and walk down the road past the drive of High Rails Farm and past the end of Woodman Wray Lane. At a cottage garden, opposite the drive of the Heights, climb left over a small stone stile into a narrow path through the garden. Straight ahead to the right-hand corner of the field and through the right-hand gate. Follow the wall to a gate and passing through this, turn right. Cross two stiles on a section of the 'Six Dales Way' to reach Hall Field House, go through the farm yard and then turn right and follow the drive to rejoin Foldshaw Lane.

17. Turn left and walk past Braithwaite C of E School. Immediately past the school, take the sign-posted footpath to the right and follow the wall through three fields. In the third field the path veers slightly left to reach a

Plumpton Gate

stone stile. Climb this and make for another stile at a section of tumble-down walling. From here, head for the corner of the wood. As you approach the wood edge a stile becomes visible. Enter the wood over this, and cross the stream at a point where there are the remains of a small bridge. The stile that was used at the beginning of the walk, below Padside Hall, is now visible. Cross this and return to the end of the drive.

Haverah Park

Distance: **10 miles**   *Map:* **OS Explorer 297**

Description: This is an easy walk with lots of interest. The first part follows the route of Short Walk 7.

Pubs: The Smiths Arms, Beckwithshaw; Sun Inn, Norwood (both slightly off route.)

Starting Point: **SE 215552**

The small parking place at the left hand side of Penny Pot Lane, to the west of Harrogate, just past Willow House.

Boundary Notes: This walk is well within the Forest, and covers the old area of Haverah Park.

---

1. Walk down the green track south from the road side. At the bottom of the lane just after it has taken a zig-zag, bear right and follow Bank Slack towards Bank End Farm.

Bank Slack is all that remains of an ancient earth works probably dating back to pre-Roman times, and most probably part of a Brigantian defensive system.

2. From Bank End Farm follow the footpath across three fields to reach the lane at a ladder stile that would take you past farm buildings towards the Sun Inn, but unless you require sustenance, do not go over this but turn left and, keeping the field wall on your right, cross two stiles to enter a field of gorse. Cross the makeshift bridge, and climb the hill ahead to reach Brown Bank Farm. Keeping the farm buildings to your left, go round them to join a footpath through a gate, and on through four fields, to pass East End

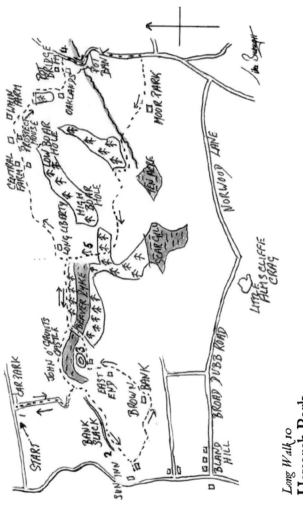

Long Walk 10
Haverah Park

Manor on your left. Go over the ladder-stile and follow the path slightly to the left and on through three small fields. There is a broken-down stone wall to your right which marks a green track. Go into the track, and follow it left, to reach the ruins of John o' Gaunt's Castle near to a complex of farm buildings, and overlooking Beaver Dyke Reservoir.

This is not a castle, but a very old Hunting Lodge, and almost certainly pre-dates John of Gaunt, who was the younger son of Edward III and was governor of Knaresborough Castle. It is thought that this hunting lodge was probably built in the reign of Edward II. Piers Gaveston, a favourite of Edward II, was granted the Liberty of Knaresborough, and Haverah Park was set up as a hunting forest within Knaresborough Forest.

3. Leave John o' Gaunt's Castle along an old green track towards the dam separating the two parts of Beaver Dyke Reservoir, and on the other side, turn right towards Long Liberty Farm. Turn left and then right, and follow the well marked track through several fields to Central House Farm and then on to Prospect House Farm. Continue straight ahead to Whin Hill Farm, and then go on through a small wood to the Oatlands, finally coming out onto the B6161 road from Killinghall to Beckwithshaw through Pot Bridge Farm.

Note the two big woods to your right as you pass through Prospect House Farm. They are called High and Low Boar Hole, and are thought to be where Thomas Ingilby, whose descendants still live at Ripley Castle, saved Edward III's life from a wild boar.

3. At the end of the wood, go through the gate and in 20 yards turn left, away from the track to Clint, along a narrow twisting footpath between hedge rows, to come out onto the road from Clint to Hampsthwaite. Turn left here to go down the metalled road to the old bridge and into Hampsthwaite.

4. Enter the village church yard and go all the way through and out by a small gate at the far end onto a flag-stoned path, which was probably part of the old Roman road. This leads out onto the Birstwith road. Turn right towards Birstwith.

Hampsthwaite is closely connected with the family of William Makepeace Thackeray, the author of 'Vanity Fair', to whom there is a memorial in the Church. Thackeray is a common name within the Knaresborough Forest, and no doubt the farm of that name, that now lies below the waters of Fewston Reservoir, and the beck that flows into it, are named after the same family.

In the village of Hampsthwaite once lived Peter Barker, an amazing 'blind joiner'. Not only could he make the finest furniture with improvised measuring tools, but he even completely rebuilt the church clock.

The original Hampsthwaite Church was built as a penance by Hugh de Moreville, once Constable of Knaresborough Castle, for his part in the murder of Thomas à Becket.

Boundary Stone 40

5. In half a mile, turn right off the road at a ruined barn, onto a marked footpath, which leads across a field to the edge of the River Nidd. Follow the Nidd upstream through some delightful woodland to enter the village of Birstwith, taking a deviation path around the flour mill. At the road, turn right towards the river and then left before crossing the bridge. The path now passes the weir and stays close to the river, until it reaches a beautiful single-arched pack-horse bridge called, ironically, New Bridge. Go over the bridge and into a narrow, walled ancient green track towards Benny Carr.

It would be worth taking a minor detour here along the river downstream to Nidd House Farm, to take a look at Stone 40, and then retracing your footsteps to rejoin the narrow track towards Benny Carr.

6. Turn right off this track before reaching the B6165 Pateley Bridge road and cross a field towards Dinmore House. Go straight across the drive of Dinmore House and, after passing the house, pick up a footpath to the left, which goes through a grassy close and then after a stile turns steeply up a

hill, past a barn, towards Burnt Yates village, keeping the old Monk Wall to your left. After two fields, each with stone stiles, enter Burnt Yates village at a stile onto the main Pateley Bridge road.

According to Speight, Grainge, and Hargrove ('Nidderdale and the Garden of the Nidd' 1894), Burnt Yates was formerly known as Bond Gate. As the village is on the boundary of the Forest, it may have gained its present name due to the Forest gates being burnt down at some time. The school in Burnt Yates was the beneficiary of three generous endowments. The first was by William Coates in 1760, and the second was from by Rear Admiral Robert Long of Winsley Hall, who left a considerable amount of land, including Flask House Farm, the income of which was to provide for the education of the poor of the township. The nearby estate of Winsley Hall was bought by the Trustees of the school in 1801 for £2,000. The third legacy, from a local man called William Mountaine in 1778, was a substantial library of Philosophical Transactions and paintings by Highmore and Maingaud, together with a collection of valuable navigational instruments invented by Mountaine himself. He had been born at a farm which, according to William Grainge, was at the bottom of Scarah Bank, and although he was completely self-taught he became one of the leading mathematicians of his age.

7. The Monk Wall continues on the opposite side of the road, but the route now turns right through the village. Take the path off to the left immediately after the school. After five fields (way-marked) the path bears left towards Cow Gate Farm. Boundary Stone 41 once stood by the beck here, but it may have disappeared at the time that new homes were built on

land that was formerly a leather mill. Follow the farm drive to reach the village of Shaw Mills.

Fountains Abbey monks had their corn milled here by a miller named Shaw, hence Shaw Mills.

8. On reaching the road, turn left and cross the bridge over Thornton Beck. The road at first curves to the right, and then at a sharp left-hand bend there is a footpath off to the right, hidden behind a crash barrier. Take the path over a small stone stile and between hedges to enter a field. The path is marked to go diagonally towards an electricity pole, but if the field is planted with a crop it is easier to follow the boundary to the right. Keeping the field fence on your right continue to a metal gate. Go straight ahead here, and at a point where there is a stile off to the right leading to a white-painted foot bridge, turn left and go up the field until in the corner you reach a wooden gate on the right.

9. Go through the gate, which is way-marked, and continue ahead, following a high-level green path with wall on your left past old oaks and hawthorn trees. The path drops down to a small field-bridge over Cold Beck, through a metal gate and on up the field, until the wall to the left turns away. Turn left with the wall and the old track, then bear round to the right and up a steep hill towards High Kettle Spring Farm. Go through the muddy farmyard, with the buildings to your left, and take the small hunting-gate on the right, with the farm house to the left. The path drops down through a small wood and past a long forgotten quarry, and continues through a small wooden gate.

The buildings on your right were formerly the Ripley village water supply, which was originally set up by Fountains Abbey. The main buildings belong to more recent times, but the small 'beehive' structure, from which the water comes, dates back many centuries. The water is good,

Boundary Stone 48

but very hard, and the spring has never been known to fail.

10. Go on to Low Kettle Spring Farm, past the pig units, and then along the drive to the Bishop Thornton road on Scarah Bank. Turn right and, when this road joins up the B6165 Pateley Bridge road, turn right again. Cross the road, go towards Pateley Bridge, and in a quarter of a mile cross Scarah Bridge (or Godwin Bridge as it was once known) and in about 50 yards take the sign-posted footpath following Ripley Park Wall to the left.

On the bank of Thornton Beck, below Scarah Bridge, Boundary Stone 42 once stood, but this disappeared with no trace within the last 20 years. By the generosity of Mr Mark Smith of HACS Civil Engineers, I have been fortunate in obtaining a suitable replacement stone, a huge former gate post of almost identical proportions to the original. Mr Smith erected the stone at a suitable nearby place in the summer of 2011. I decided that, as the original position was on private land, a better position would be about 100 yards further along the side of Ripley Park wall. More people will be able to see it as they pass on the public right of way towards High Rails Farm at Whipley. The exact position was chosen because it is in a direct line from Stones 44 and 43 to Stone 42's original position at Scarah Bridge, where the line meets the Ripley Park wall. Mr Andrew Walmsley of Scarah Bank Farm kindly agreed to permit the new stone to be placed on his land. The inscription, by a local stonemason, has 42 at the top, K F below, and under that 2010, as it was felt deceitful to put 1767, and the fact that Stones 8 and 9 are marked 1825 provides a precedent.

11. Continue up the field and through a gate into the next field, to the point where the park wall veers off slightly left. At this point continue straight ahead. Close to a large oak tree stands Boundary Stone 43, and 100 yards on and a little to the right at the other side of a wood and wire fence, stands Boundary Stone 44, both at a rakish angle.

There are several large oak trees in this area, and it is likely that they all come from acorns from a huge oak that grew at this spot, known as the Godwin Oak, which is mentioned in both the 1576 and the 1767 Boundary Perambulations. The old name 'Godwin Bridge' also comes from this tree.

12.   Return now to the park wall and follow it to two kissing gates.   Go through to join the lane that follows the park wall towards Saddlers Barn.

After only a few yards the wall top dips a couple of courses of stones. Look over the wall at this low place and, across about 30 yards of tree felling debris, notice an unusual standing stone. It is thought by some to be the Monk Cross that formerly stood at the upper end of Dog Lane near the fork at Whipley, while others think it could be Corpse Cross. There are several theories about it, including the possibility that it could be the burial place of the Danish thane Archil.

13.   Now follow the park wall to join the bridle track from Ripley and, keeping the wall on your left, return to the village and your car.

Note as you go the magnificent views of Ripley Castle across the lake, and then as you cross the old mill bridge by the lake outflow, look over the other side of the bridge to see a tiny stone building. This was a water-powered turbine, supplying electricity to the castle. It was still operational until about 1960, looked after by Mr Harry Thorpe, whose family had lived in the village for generations. Many large ancestral homes had their own electricity supply before the National Grid was established.

Now as you walk up the hill towards the village, notice a series of mounds and hollows in the field just below the garden wall of York House. These are now thought to be the remains of a Victorian ornamental garden.

Long Walk *12*
Ripley - Nidd Valley - Spruisty

Distance: **7.5 miles**   *Map:* **OS Explorer 289**

Description: The Nidd Gorge can be muddy in winter but it is a wonderful area. Just do it!

Pubs: The Three Horse Shoes, Killinghall; the Gardeners Arms, Old Bilton.

Starting Point: **SE 287597**

Killinghall Bridge, on the A61 between Killinghall and Ripley. The bridge is now by-passed by a high-level bridge, and parking is usually easy. There is a good bus service from Harrogate to Ripon and a bus stop nearby.

Boundary Notes: In this area the Boundary follows the River Nidd.

1.   On the north (Ripley) side of the bridge, follow the river Nidd downstream, through an area of small hills with large mature beech trees. The hills are earth that was discarded when the railway to Pateley Bridge was built. Continue downstream and, soon after passing a large island in the river, bear left towards a stile and join the recently reopened cycle route, which was originally the Nidd Valley railway line, closed by Dr Beeching in the 1960s. Turn right on this and, a short distance after the track bends right, cross what was the railway viaduct over the river. On the other side of this, go left, drop down to the river side and follow the river downstream.

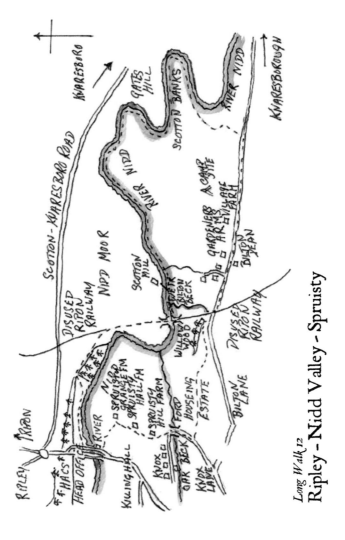

The path here is easy to follow, as it is a designated footpath, the Harrogate Ringway. The path from the viaduct passes the steep-sided valley of Bilton Beck and in less than a mile a large weir.

> *The property on the opposite side was Scotton corn mill. A little further down in a clearing of the woodland there still remain the humps and bumps of the mill race of the ancient Bilton Corn Mill. In the days of Knaresborough Forest, Bilton was a particularly important place, as it had specific responsibility for the care of one of the Forest's designated forest areas, Bilton Park. The forest pale had to be regularly repaired and the Bilton people were required to do it. There still remains a small section of the original pale on the land of Bilton Village Farm. This park, and Haverah Park near Beckwithshaw, were used for the maintenance of game stock and horses.*

2. Continue downstream now for two and three quarter miles, to reach the unmade part of Bilton Lane. Turn right, ignoring the sign left for the Harrogate Ringway. Follow Bilton Lane to Old Bilton and, a few yards past the Gardeners Arms, turn right onto the old bed of the Harrogate to Ripon Railway. In a short distance a path, once the narrow-gauge Gas Works railway, leaves this on the left, and passes to the left of Willow Wood. Continue along this to enter Old Trough Way. At the road junction, turn right until reaching Knox Lane. Go right and follow the road to Oak Beck by a delightful pack horse-bridge called Spruisty Bridge.

3. Cross the road ahead and go up a flight of steps to the left of the arched drive entrance. At the top, continue along the bottom edge of a garden and up a narrow path to a stile. Climb this into a field and head slightly left to a stile. Go over this and keep on the same heading to another stile in the top

left-hand corner of the field. Go straight ahead to cross over the drive of Spruisty Hill Farm. Pass the farm close on your right and reach the drive of Spruisty Hall Farm.

The name Spruisty comes from the family called Spructoe, who originally lived here during the reign of Charles II. Nearby Spruisty Grange was once owned by William Sheepshanks, a former benefactor of Harrogate.

4. Follow the drive up to the farm yard and go left through a sign-posted gate. Keeping the farm buildings on your right, go to a field gate and immediately left over a stile. Go diagonally across this field towards Spruisty Grange. Walk past the Grange and follow the edge of the field with the hedge to your left. At the field boundary ahead there is a plank bridge over a dike. Aim towards the big house ahead and over the stiles with gates on the top. The next field is a narrow one, and then turn diagonally left to the corner, and out onto an extremely muddy farm lane known locally as Pickersgill Lane. Follow the lane to the left, and then where it goes right leave it by going straight on. Keep going straight on and in the left-hand corner of this field there is a stile with a path that leads down to the old road from Killinghall Bridge. Go right and reach the starting point of the walk.

The Weir on the Nidd by the bridge once powered the Killinghall corn mill. It was a powerful mill with two waterwheels. It, like many of the corn mills of the Forest, was converted into a flax and linen mill, and was tragically demolished in the 1970s to make way for a modern house.

A Very
Long Walk

Perambulation of the Forest Boundary

The Forest Boundary, as described in the Last Perambulation, is around 90 miles in length. It is a long-held dream of mine that some day it will form the basis of a long-distance walk, visiting the various Boundary Stones along the way. To this end, the route of the Boundary, broken into seven sections, is described below, and you can see it in the Map of the Forest which is repeated here, with the sites of the remaining Boundary Stones indicated. With the aid of the excellent Ordnance Survey Explorer Series of 1:25000 maps (you will need numbers 289, 297 and 298), and by following nearby rights of way, and using "permissive paths" or "access land", a series of linear walks close to or on the Boundary could be worked out, and for energetic and experienced walkers, it would be straightforward to convert each of these sections into a (very long!) circular walk of 20 miles or so, or eventually to string them together to make your own Perambulation, visiting the Boundary Stones along the way. If you want to see each Stone, Appendix 1 gives a more detailed list, with their exact grid references, and elevations above sea level. However, as some of them are on private land you must request access to view them from the landowners concerned. Contact details for this are also given in Appendix 1, but I have deliberately avoided giving phone numbers, so that only those who seriously need to visit otherwise inaccessible Boundary Stones will be likely to take the trouble to request access.

Opposite: Haxby Hippings

The Forest of Knaresborough

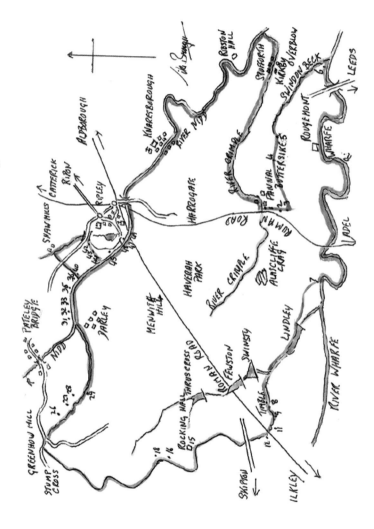

All but two of the 12 Short Walks, and the 12 Long Walks described in this book, run along, or close to, sections of the Boundary, and pass several of the Boundary Stones, and they could form a basis for a Boundary Walk. The Walks' locations in relation to the Boundary sections are given below, with a note of which Stones can be seen en route. The Walks that do not run along the Boundary are Short Walk 7, and Long Walk 10, as these are well within the Forest, north of the Boundary, and west of Harrogate, and cover the ancient area of the Forest known as Haverah Park.

Section 1
Confluence of the Rivers Nidd and Crimple to Pannal
GR: SE405531 to SE304514

The Perambulation historically begins at the confluence of the River Nidd with the River Crimple (SE405531). From here the Boundary follows the Crimple upstream, passing to the south of Ribston, and bends south and then west, to reach the outskirts of Spofforth, where the Crimple forms a big arc to the north, before bending south again to reach the outskirts of Harrogate at Pannal. Here is the first Boundary Stone, Stone 1 (SE3045140), at the point where the Buttersyke enters the Crimple.

Short Walk 1 is around Ribston, and touches the River Nidd, which forms part of the Boundary here.

Long Walk 1 takes a wider circle north and west of Ribston, passing near to the north bank of the River Nidd.

Short Walk 2 follows the Crimple from Hookstone Wood to Pannal, passing Stone 1, and it would be possible to add Stones 2 and 3 to the start of this walk.

Short Walk 3 starts at Hookstone Ponds, and crosses the Boundary twice as it circles through Pannal. From Bathing Well Wood to Collin Bridge, the route is close to the Boundary.

Long Walk 2 starts at Follifoot south-east of Harrogate, includes a section along the River Crimple as it flows towards Pannal, and the same section of Boundary from Bathing Well Wood to Collin Bridge as Short Walk 2.

Section 2
Pannal to Castley
GR SE304514 to SE262460

From Stone 1 at Pannal, the Boundary runs south-west for a half a mile or so to Stone 2, and then swings south-east, past Stones 3, 4 and 5 to Warholes, where it meets the Baffle (or Swindon) Beck (SE 314495). The Boundary follows the beck downstream, (but this is not a right of way) to the confluence with the Wharfe, the probable site of Stone 6, now missing. The Wharfe is then followed upstream, to reach Stone 7 on the road side close to Castley Ings Farm Drive.

Long Walk 3 crosses the Baffle Beck a couple of times south of Kirkby Overblow, and then follows the Wharfe upstream.

Short Walk 4 starts at Castley, near Stone 7, and circles to the north of the Boundary.

Section 3
Castley to Timble Gill
GR SE262460 to SE171528

From Stone 7 the Boundary follows the edge of Riffa Wood to Stainburn and then goes along the Thrispin Beck (not a right of way) to reach the

Washburn (SE 230461). It then follows the Washburn upstream, passing the modern reservoir of Lindley Wood. At the junction with the stream of Timble Gill the Boundary turns west, to follow it as far as Stone 8.

Long Walk 4 circles to the east of Lindley Wood Reservoir.
Short Walk 5 is in the area of Timble Gill and Swinsty Reservoir.
Short Walk 6 goes along the Washburn and Timble Gill.
Long Walk 5 is a wider circle to the north of Timble Gill, around Swinsty and Fewston Reservoirs.

Section 4
Timble Gill to Cort Howe
GR SE171528 to SE100575

From Stone 8 the Boundary then leaves the Timble Gill stream for the moors, climbing in a west-north-westerly direction, and passing Stones 9 to 12. The Boundary continues on its way to cross the A59 road at Pace Beck (SE117548). From here a little stream, the Black Sike, leads north-west to Cort (or Carle) Howe. Stone 15, that used to be here, is now built into the doorstep of the nearby Rocking Hall Shooting Lodge.

Long Walk 6 follows the Boundary along the stretch from Stone 9 to Stone 12.
Long Walk 7 reaches Rocking Hall from Blubberhouses at the head of Fewston Reservoir.

Section 5
Cort Howe to Padside Hall
GR SE100575 to SE 148603

At Cort Howe the Boundary takes a sharp turn roughly to the north, to a point slightly north of Harden Head, where Boundary Stone 16 can be found. From here the Boundary passes north-west, to Lord's Seat, where a large rock serves as Stone 18, and then roughly north-north-east, to Keld Houses. This stretch of Boundary was re-aligned in 1809 because of a dispute between Sir Thomas White of Eagle Hall and Sir Thomas Yorke of Gouthwaite Hall over its exact location. Stones 21, 22, 23, 24 and 25 are all missing and it is understood that they were 'cast down' during this dispute. The Boundary now turns south-east, along the small beck called Greenhow Sike. Stones 26, 27 (built into a dry stone wall close to High House Farm) and 28 are quite close together, leading to the headwaters of Folly (or Padside) beck, where from the bridge near Padside Hall Stone 29 can be seen. There is an old right of way that passes Stone 29, but permission to view closer is required.

Long Walk 8 circles south from Keld Houses to Lords Seat and Stone 18.
Short Walk 10 is around Padside Hall.
Long Walk 9 takes a wider circle around Padside Hall, passing Stone 29.

Section 6
Padside Hall to Ripley and Stone 49
GR SE 148603 to SE 283599

From Padside Hall the Boundary follows the beck east, as it becomes Darley Beck, and eventually empties into the River Nidd at SE205601. A string of Stones (31, 32, 33, 35, 36 and 38) follows the north bank of the

Nidd to Stone 40. Here the Boundary leaves the river, turning north in a big loop to follow the Monks Wall to Burnt Yates, and Shaw Mills, where Stone 41 once stood. The boundary curves round to run south-south-west, past the replica of Stone 42, which has been placed by the wall of Ripley Park in line with the Stones 43 and 44, and runs south past Stone 45 to the River Nidd. Stone 48 is on the river bank, but Stone 49, the final Boundary Stone, lies to the north of the present river, on the course of an old meander.

Short Walk 9 is west of Darley, along the Darley Beck, and near to its confluence with the Nidd.

Long Walk 10 is a wider circle west of Darley, along the Darley Beck.

Short Walk 8 circles south of the River Nidd, east of Darley.

Short Walk 12 is to the west of Ripley and passes nearby Stones 42 to 44.

Long Walk 11 is a wider circle from Ripley, and follows the Boundary for a considerable distance, along the Nidd and the Monks Wall, passing Stones 40, 42, 43, 44 and 45.

Section 7
Stone 49 near Ripley to the Crimple
GR SE 283599 to SE405531

The old meander reaches the current course of the Nidd again close to Killinghall Bridge, and the river is then followed downstream, past Knaresborough, all the way to the confluence with the Crimple, where our journey started.

Short Walk 11 is a linear walk along the Nidd from Harrogate to Knaresborough.
Long Walk 12 is circular, but follows the Nidd from Killinghall Bridge downstream before turning back via Spruisty.

Appendices

List of Appendices

Appendix 1
List of Boundary Stones

tone	Marking	Grid Reference	Elevation	Notes
1	KF 1767	SE 30354 51409	287 ft	Where the Buttersyke joins the Crimple.
2	KF 1767	SE 30022 50764	343 ft	Close to the road bridge over the railway at Burn Bridge. Permission from: Mr. Carling, Horn Bank Farm, North Rigton, Harrogate
3	KF 1767	SE 30287 49923	367 ft	In a field on the west side of the Leeds to Harrogate road, where there is often a car boot sale.
4	KF 1767	SE 31321 49619	473 ft	At the top of the twisting hill on Walton Head Lane, in the hedge of the right.
5	KF 1767	SE 31319 49537	470 ft	Fifty yards across the field behind Stone 4 in the close called Warholes Well. Permission from Mr Douthwaite, High Snape Farm, Kirkby Overblow, Harrogate.
6		SE 33119 46705		Stone missing, probably at the bottom of the river. Long Walk 3.
7	KF 1767	SE 26205 46059	157 ft	On roadside, only the top of the stone remains visible.
8	KF 1823	SE 17092 52794	738 ft	At Sowerbarge Field, at a bend on the Blubberhouses to Otley Road. The date suggests that this stone, and stone 9, were replaced. Re-erected in 1998 by Cyril Mason and John Webster. Difficult to spot, as behind a large bush.
9	KF 1823	SE 15948 52270	971 ft	Ellercarr Pike. Long Walk 6
10	Missing	Est. SE 151 524	Est. 1000ft	Known to exist, but difficult to find in the heather.
11	KF 1767	SE 14345 52477	1089 ft	Close to the shooting shelter on Lippersley Edge. Long Walk 6
12	KF 1767, also F but no number	SE 13311 53001	1076 ft	Earthbound and the base stone of a gatepost. Close to the very ancient milepost on the old Roman Road. Long Walk 6
13		Not Found		At Pace House Beck
14		Not Found. Est. SE 10853 57600		At the foot of Black Syke
15	KF 1767	SE 11046 57854	1297 ft	Now built into the shooting lodge as a door step at Rocking Hall. Long Walk 7

Stone	Marking	Grid Reference	Elevation	Notes
16	KF 1767	SE 09477 58984	1230 ft	The stone is lying down, but with its engraved sid facing up, at Harden Head.
17		Not found. Est. SE 08595 59880		Probably sunk into the peat at Dry Tarn.
18	KF 1767	SE 08499 59938	1542 ft	Cut upon a huge rock at Lord's Seat. Long Walk
19		Not Found		At Armshaw Gill Head
20		Not Found		Long Walk 8
21 25		Missing		Stones 21 to 25 were said to have been cast down during the dispute in 1809 over lead between Sir Thomas White and Sir Thomas Yorke, which le to the re-alignment of the boundary
26	KF 1767	SE 13796 61416	1100 ft	Close to Palleys Crags and Jordan Bog. Long Wa 9
27	KF 1767	SE 13839 61166	1077 ft	On its side, facing out of the dry stone wall at Hi House Farm near Palleys Crags. Permission from the Sheepshanks, High House Farm, Summerbridge, Harrogate. Call 01423 781711
28	KF 1767	SE 14113 60849	1036 ft	At High Burns, on a hump of ground near a grou of trees.
29	KF 1767	SE 14786 60294	873 ft	In a field on the left of the drive of Padside Hall, and close to the beck. Permission from: Mr. Moorhouse, Burns Farm, Summerbridge, Harrogate. Long Walk 9
30		Lost .Est. SE 4646 0095		Probably lost when the Nidd Valley Railway was built.
31	Only 31 visible	SE 20989 59755	268 ft	The north side of the river Nidd, where the field boundary from White Oak joins the river. Long Walk 10
32	Only 32 visible	SE 21181 59723	261 ft	On the north side if the river Nidd between the footpath from the footbridge to the track leading from Haxby Hippings. Long Walk 10
33	KF1767	SE 21210 59724	272 ft	To the east of the above track on the north bank the Nidd. Permission from: Mr. M. Smith, HA Ltd., The Old Railway Station, Ripley, Harrogat Long Walk 10
34		Not found		Probably buried on the river bank in its original position. Permission as Stone 33

Stone	Marking	Grid Reference	Elevation	Notes
35	KF 1767	SE 21622 59839	259 ft	North bank of the Nidd. Permission as Stone 33. Long Walk 10
36	KF 1767	SE 22181 60050		The north bank of the Nidd in the field between the river and the old railway embankment. Permission from: Mrs. H. Patrick, Flo's Farm, Hartwith, Summerbridge, Harrogate.
37		Not found		May have been lost in the river
38	KF 1767	SE 22741 60241	238 ft	The north bank of the Nidd, near to Ross Toll Bridge. Permission as Stone 36 above.
39		Not found		
40	KF 1767	SE 24056 60172	220 ft	Near to Nidd House Farm. Permission from: Mr Holmes, Nidd House Farm Birstwith, Harrogate. Long Walk 11
41		Missing		Once stood at Shaw Mills near to Cow Gate Farm.
42	KF 2010	SE 27538 61558	206 ft	This Stone is a replacement of the original that went missing around 1990. Long Walk 11; Short Walk 12
43	KF 1767	SE 27012 61114	339 ft	Ripley Park wall side. Long Walk 11; Short Walk 12
44	KF 1767	SE 26950 61066	365 ft	Ripley Park wall side. Long Walk 11; Short Walk 12
45	KF 1767	SE 26935 59983	242 ft	At the gate where the unmade lane from Clint to Ripley enters Holly Bank Wood.
46		Missing		Might have stood where the small beck from Holly Bank Wood meets the Nidd. Permission from: Mr. C. Parker, Hark Hill Nook, Clint, Harrogate.
47	KF 1767	Estimated SE 284 597		At the point where the old meander leaves the present course of the river. Permission from: Mr. A. Binns, Bungalow Farm, Clint, Hampsthwaite, Harrogate. Access is through HACS yard, and will also require permission from Mr. M. Smith, HACS Ltd., The Old Railway Station, Ripley, Harrogate.
48	KF 1767	SE 28039 59548	170 ft	Lying down, but face up, in the old dry river bed. Permissions as Stone 47.
49	KF 1767	SE 28345 59887	181 ft	On the old meander, at the side of what is now Ripley Beck No Access.

Appendix 2
Some Known Perambulations

Reign	Title	Date	Notes
Edward II	Perambulation	1325	Probably not undertaken fully
Elizabeth I	Perambulation	1577	Some boundary stones still exist
James I	Survey	1613	
Charles I	Perambulation	1623	
Cromwell	Survey & Agreement	1651	
Last Perambulation		1767	Most stones still exist and are numbered
Copy holders Perambulation		1770	Several stones remain in changed boundary

Appendix 3
The Elizabethan Perambulation
20ᵗʰ August 1576

The Metes and Bounders of the perambulation of Her Majesty's Forrest of Knaresburgh begin at the River Nidd where the Cremple enters into Nidd, and so up Cremple to the Black Stones lying in Blackstonwath, a ford in Cremple on the way leading from Ribstone to Ingmanthorp; thence up Cremple to Stock-bridge, on the highway from Spofforth to Deighton, between Ribstone and Wetherby; thence up Cremple to Oxenbridge; thence to Pannal; thence to Buttersike; thence by a dry ditch to a syke called Doubledyke, coming from Walton Head Lane in the church way, between Rigton and Kirkby Overblows; thence directly through a close called Waroholes to a well there called Warchele-well, out of which Swindon-sike springs. Then down Swindon Sike to Bawgehell yate in the highway to Wetherby out of the west country, which Swindon-sike divides the Forrest of Knaresburgh and the Lordship of Kirkby Overblows; so from Bawghell or Baugh-yate following the syke to the Midstream of the Wharfe to the west side of Castley-yugs, and so up a lane abounding upon the end of a little brook called Dead Water End, at a close there called Deadwater. So over the west side of Castley Lordship to Riffoe Wood, and by that woodside to Riffoe yate; thence to a close called Buckrodes, parcel of the Lordship of Stayneburne, and by the side of that close to Riffoe becke, and up that beck leaving the bounder between Stainburn and Leathley-more to Cromock-hole; thence up Staynburne field side by a little sike coming from Thrissen , and so to Stonewath-yate and by Staynburne field side, as Thrissen leads west to the south-west end of Stainburn field; then directly to Swanken-well, alias Sweinrode-kell, which well is a little south from a great stone with three holes in it. And as the way lying adjoining on the north side of that well leads to Holbecke, so down Holbecke to Washburn, so up Washburn to the foot of Ridgemond becke to the foot of Timble gill becke, so to the south end of Sowerbargh lane end and so following a sike to the corner of Sowerbargh field, and so up an old dyke to the milne pond and by the same dyke to a place called Standing-stone on the Crosse ridge, so up that ridge to Dunocksboure, and so to Lepsley Pike; thence to Gawkhall ridge, and so up to Mekellgill head and by the over end of Loftshaw gill to Fanas carr (Fawsber pike) above Beamsley; thence to skarre above Inkhorn-gill (Ickeringill) house on the west part of the Queen's fold, so up Pacehouse becke to the Black sike, and up that sike to Carle-howe end; thence to Hardin head, and so to the south side of Dry tarn; thence to the Lord's seat, and so down the hill by the south side of Gowland Maw, then by a little sike unto Oxgill, and following that gill to the lower end of Middle Tong towards Appletreewick; thence up Armeshaw gill to Lyard yate, and following that gill to the head thereof; thence to the top of a hill called Roarer-louts, and so over Munga gill to a place where Craven Crosse stood over against the end of Munga gill, and thence to Craven keld by the highway from Hebden to Pattlay briggs; thence following that way to Grenehow hill, and by the skirts of the South side of the hill to a way leading to Ripley, and by this same way to the head of Grenehow sike between Cawdstones and Ridlish; thence down the sike to Plumpton Gayt, and following the gayt to Pallitt stones (Pallice Stones) (Abbots Hand); thence to the end of an old dike in Braithwaite, so to Padside becke, and from it as the Monk wall leads upon the south side of Nidd to the river of Nidd, and directly over Nidd to the said wall on the north side of that river; and so as the Monk wall leads on the north side of that river to Wrecke holme, and still following the wall to Bunt Yate standing on the highway between Brinbom, alias Brynham and Ripley; so to the Cowgate in the Monk wall end and by that wall to Thornton becke, which divides the Lordship of Thornton and the Forrest of Knaresburgh; so down that water to a wath called Skarne Wath, a bounder between the Forest and the Lord Archbishop of York and the Lordship of Ripley; so down the water to Godswaine bridge at Sharrow Mill, then up a little sike called Black sike, running on the outside of Rypley Parke payle to Godwaine dyke unto Gawdewane Oke; and so as the same dike leads which runs in most places without the parke, and in some places near unto the payle within the parke, to the Crosse called Muncke Head at Ripley Parke yate in Whipley lane end; so by the same pale down a lane called Dogg lane, alias Esh lane, alias Whipley Lane, and to stone called Cap Crosse at Ripley Park side in the end of a lane from Clint to Ripley; so down by Robert Woodside by a little sike to the river Nidd, and so down that river to the nether end of Sawcroft, the inheritance of Sir William Ingilby, Knight, where the old course of the Nidd has been; and following the old course of the river by a close called the lady Sawcroft parcel of the Lordship of Ripley to the Nidd again, and down the river to Killinghall Bridge, and still descending the river to the place mentioned where Cremple comes into Nidd at Ribstan.

The jurors say upon their oaths that all the places and bounders before specified are true bounders of the perambulation of Her Majesty's Forest of Knaresburgh, as to them either by riding with the said commissioners about the perambulation of the Forest to see and view all the said places, or by diligent search and examination amongst the most ancient men there dwelling to learn the true bounders thereof, or as by any record to them showed, or by any other way or means whatsoever at this present may or can appear.

In witness thereof as well as the said commissioners as the jurors have hereunto put their hands and seals the day and year above –written.

Appendix 4
The Last Perambulation
15TH *July 1767/ 8* *Completed 22nd January 1768*

The Metes & Boundaries of his Majesty's Forest of Knaresborough begin at the Stream of the River Nidd, where the Rivulet, called Crimple, runs into the said River; at which Place, the said Crimple is bounded, on or towards the South, by a Parcel of enclosed Land, in the Manor of North Deighton, belonging to Sir John Ingilby, Bart., called Tomling-Ing: and, on or towards the North, by Part of the enclosed Land belonging to Henry Pullein, called Black-Stones, lying in the township of Little-Ribston, (which said Little-Ribston is in the Boundary of the said Forest); and from thence, ascending up the Stream of the Crimple to Blackstone - Wath, over which the Road from Ribston to Ingmanthorp leadeth; and so along the Stream of Crimple, to the South East Corner of Ribston-Moor, commonly called Ribston-Green; and from thence, up the Stream of Crimple, to a Piece or Parcel of Ground formally an Island, in the Lordship of North-Deighton, called Mill-Green, and Mill-

Paddock, being the place where North-Deighton Mill formally stood; and so along the North side of Mill-Green, and Mill-Paddock, being the ancient Course of Crimple, to a Bridge, called Crimple-Bridge, over which, the Road from Ribston to Wetherby leadeth; and from thence along the Stream of Crimple, which still divides the Lordship of North-Deighton, on or towards the South from the said Ribston-Green, lying within the Boundary of the said Forest, on or towards the North, to the South-West corner of the said Ribston-Green; thence along the Stream of Crimple, where it divides the Lordship of North-Deighton, on or towards the South, from the enclosed Lands, within the Township of Ribston, aforesaid; on or towards the North, so to Stock-Bridge, otherwise, Newsam-Bridge, over which the road from Spofforth to North-Deighton leadeth; and from thence , along the Stream of Crimple, where it leads by the East, South, and West Sides of a certain parcel of enclosed Land, called Newsam, belonging to Sir John Ingilby and lying within the Boundary of the said Forest, to Point-Bridge; over which the Turnpike Road from Wetherby, through Spofforth To Knaresborough leadeth; and from thence along the Stream of Crimple, to Oxen-Bridge near Spofforth Mill; and from thence along the Stream of Crimple to Guildhouse-Bridge, over which the Road from Plumpton to Follyfoot leads; and from thence along the Stream of Crimple, to Follyfoot-Wath over which the Carriage Road from Plumpton to Follyfoot Leadeth; when the open Forest begins; and from thence proceeding up the Stream of Crimple, to a Bridge, called Collin-Bridge, formally a Horse Bridge, but lately made a Carriage Bridge; and from thence, along the Stream of Crimple, the said open Forest lying on or towards the North, and the Township of Follyfoot, on or towards the South, to a certain Hill or Island, whereon a Mill, for smelting Iron Ore, formally stood, and now called Mill-Hill, and thence along the Stream of Crimple , by Fulwith-Mill, to Almsford-Wath, where a Bridge is now built, over which, the Turnpike Road from Leeds to Ripley leadeth; and from thence, still along the Stream of Crimple, by

Pannel-Mill to the foot of a certain Dyke, which runs into Crimple called Buttersyke; and from thence turning Southward and following the said Syke, where it divides the Township of Rigton, lying within the boundary of the said Forest, on or towards the West, from the lands of Walton Head, on or towards the East, to a small Bridge or Drain, through which the water of the same Syke runneth; and along the said Syke, to the North-East corner of Buttersyke Intake, beloging to Daniel Lascelles, Esquire and from thence to the Head of Buttersyke, where the 4 stones, mentioned in the ancient Boundary, formally stood; and thence again cross the said Turnpike Road leading from Leeds to Ripley, Southwards to Dry-Dyke, dividing the lands of Swindon, belonging to _____ Bethel, Esq.; on or towards the West, from the open Common of Walton-Head, on or towards the East; and from thence, to a Syke, sometimes called Double-Dyke, coming from Walton-Head; and so up the same Syke, to a Place in Walton-Head Lane, being the Church way from Rigton to Kirkby-Overblow; at which place, 2 Stones, mentioned in the ancient Boundary, formally stood; and from thence directly through a Close, called Wareholes, to a Well called Wareholes Well, out of which Swindon Syke springeth; and so down Swindon Syke, to Bow-Yate, standing in the High-Road which leads out of the West Country to Wetherby, which Swindon-Syke divides the Lordship of Swindon on the West, being within the Boundary of the said Forest, and the Lordship of Kirkby-Overblow, on or towards the East; and from the said Bowhill-Yate, following the same Syke to the middle of the River Wharfe, dividing the lands on or towards the West, in the Township of Dun-Keswick, being within the Boundary of the said Forest, from the Lands on or towards the East, in the township of Keerby-cum Netherby; and from thence turning West ward, and ascending up the middle of the Stream of Wharfe, to Harewood-Bridge, over which the said Turnpike Road from Leeds to Ripley, leadeth; The Lands in the Township of the said Dun-Keswick, adjoining upon the North Side of the River; and from thence still ascending up the Middle of the Stream of Wharfe, where the Lands of Dun-Keswick, Weeton, and Casly, likewise adjoin on the North Side of the said River, to the West Side of Casly-Ings; and so along the Lane, across a small Rill of Water, called Dead-Water, runneth; and out of the said Lane, into and over the Westward Side of Dead-Water Close, and several other Closes, which form the West Side of Casly Township, adjoin upon a part of Leathley Lordship, to Riffoe-Wood, and so by the East Side of Riffoe-Wood , to Riffoe-Yate; and from thence, into and over a Close in Stainburn Lordship, called Buck-Roods, to Riffoe-Beck, is the Boundary between Stainburn and Leathley-Moor; and from thence, along the same Beck, to a Breach in the Ground, called Crammock-Hole; and from thence up the Bech there, called Thrissen-Syke, which said Syke divides Stainburn-Field and Leathley-Moor, so to the South-West Corner of the said Field, (now enclosed and divided) by which Corner the Turnpike Road from Bradford to Ripley leads, and near which, on Leathley-Moor, (now also enclosed) is a Boggy Place, called Thrispen, otherwise Thrissen-Head, out of which the Syke there called Thrissen-Syke, and afterwards Riffoe-Beck springeth; and from thence to Swankin-Well, otherwise Swanrood Keld, which springeth a little South from a great Stone with 3 Holes in it; and from thence, by the Syke coming from the said Well (where was formally a Road, but changed at the enclosing of the said Stainburn-Field) to Holbeck, and so down Holbeck to the Stream of Washburn, and so up Washburn to Lipley-Wath, otherwise Lipersley-Wath: The Township of Lindley within the Boundary of the said Forest, being on or towards the North, and the Township of Farnley, on or towards the South; and from thence, up Washburn, to Dog-Park Bridge; and from thence, to the foot of Ridgeman-Beck; and so up the same Beck, to the foot of Timble-Gill Beck; and so ascending up a Branch of the said Beck, to the end of Sewerbarge-Lane, and following the said Branch there, called a Syke, to the South West Corner of Sewerbarge-Field, which Field is in the Township of Timble; and from thence turning Southward by an old Syke (upon which Syke Part of an old Cottage